SINGLE PARENTING

ALISHA CORREA

SINGLE PARENTING

COMPREHENSIVE STRATEGIES, PERSONAL
EMPOWERMENT, AND BUILDING RESILIENT
FAMILIES – A SURVIVAL GUIDE FOR THE SINGLE
PARENT IN TODAY'S WORLD

Abstract
publishers

"Being a single parent is twice the work, twice the stress and twice the tears but also twice the hugs, twice the love and twice the pride."

— Unknown

Table of Contents

Introduction

Imagine yourself standing in the kitchen, preparing dinner for your child while simultaneously attempting to manage work emails, help with homework, and soothe your toddler's tantrum. It's just another day in the life of a single parent, and you can't help but feel overwhelmed and exhausted. As you finally sink into the couch, exhausted and feeling the weight of your responsibilities, you can't help but wonder how other single parents manage to balance it all.

Did you know that in the United States alone, nearly 14 million single parents are raising over 21 million children? That's nearly one in every four families headed by a single parent. Despite these staggering numbers, single parents often face unique challenges, from financial struggles to social stigma, making their parenting journey even more difficult.

This book is here to change that narrative. With this practical guide, you'll learn how to navigate the unique challenges of solo parenting, embrace your strengths, build a supportive network, and raise happy, resilient children.

You will no longer feel alone or overwhelmed – instead, you'll be empowered to create a thriving environment for you and your children.

As a single parent, you face numerous problems and challenges daily that can be both physically and emotionally draining. You may often be overwhelmed by the responsibility of raising your children alone. Your days are filled with constant multitasking as you try to balance work, household chores, and your children's needs, all without the support of a partner.

Finding a support network can also be a significant challenge for single parents. It's not uncommon to feel isolated, as if no one around you truly understands the unique demands of solo parenting. This sense of loneliness can be compounded by the judgment or stigmatization you might face from others who don't appreciate the strength and dedication required to be a single parent.

Financial challenges are another concern for single parents as they strive to provide for their children's needs on a single income. This can mean making tough decisions about work, childcare, and even housing while ensuring your children have the best possible opportunities for a bright future.

Amidst these difficulties, many single parents also grapple with guilt and self-doubt, questioning their ability to be a good parent without a partner. This emotional turmoil can be exacerbated by societal expectations and the pressure to meet your children's needs in every aspect of their lives.

Understanding these problems and pain points is crucial to finding solutions and support tailored to the unique experience of single parenting. The "Single Parenting" guide provides the guidance and resources needed to overcome these obstacles and empower single parents to create a nurturing environment for their children.

By reading this book, you'll discover a wealth of benefits specifically designed to address the unique challenges of solo parenting. The book offers practical strategies and tips to empower you to become a more effective and confident single parent.

One of this book's primary benefits is its guidance on building a solid support network. You'll learn how to forge connections with other single parents, seek out resources within your community, and create a circle of friends and family who understand and support your journey. This will help alleviate feelings of isolation and loneliness while providing valuable advice, encouragement, and camaraderie.

The book also focuses on helping you achieve a healthier work-life balance. You'll gain insights into managing your time and energy more effectively, setting priorities, and delegating tasks when necessary. These strategies will not only ease your stress and prevent burnout but also ensure you can dedicate quality time to your children and create lasting memories together.

Financial challenges are also addressed with practical advice on budgeting, saving, and making the most available resources. You'll learn how to navigate the economic landscape as a single parent, ensuring you can provide for your children's needs without sacrificing their future opportunities.

Another significant benefit of the "Single Parenting" guide is its focus on emotional well-being. The book offers guidance on overcoming guilt and self-doubt, teaching you to embrace your strengths and celebrate your achievements as a single parent. You'll also find tips for fostering resilience in your children, helping them develop the skills and mindset needed to thrive in adversity.

As the author of this book, I bring a wealth of personal and professional experience to guide and support you on your journey as a single parent. My experience as a single parent has taught me firsthand the challenges and triumphs of this unique role. I have navigated the often-overwhelming responsibilities of raising children on my own, balancing work and family life, and faced the financial hurdles accompanying single parenthood. Through it all, I have learned invaluable lessons and gained insights I am eager to share with others in similar situations.

In addition to my personal experience, I have spent years working with families and children in various capacities. This background has allowed me to develop a deep understanding of child development, family dynamics, and the specific needs of single-parent families. Through my work, I have helped countless single parents build the skills and resilience to raise their children in a loving, supportive environment.

I have spent years researching and compiling resources tailored to single parents, from support groups and community programs to financial assistance options. My dedication to helping single parents has led me to advocate for their needs and challenges. I have even been featured as a guest speaker at various events and conferences focused on single-parent families.

With my unique blend of personal experience, professional expertise, and unwavering passion for supporting single parents, I am well-equipped to guide you on your journey to single parenting success.

I aim to empower you with practical solutions, insights, and resources that will enable you to confidently embrace your role as a single parent and create a thriving, supportive environment for you and your children. I am committed to helping you overcome the unique obstacles of solo parenting and celebrate your strengths as you raise happy, resilient children.

1. The World of Single Parenting

As you navigate the demanding world of single parenting, you may find yourself searching for guidance, support, and understanding from someone who has been there and knows exactly what you're going through. This guide is specifically designed for single parents like you, addressing the unique challenges, emotions, and obstacles you face daily.

By choosing this book, you're investing in practical advice, actionable strategies, and a compassionate, empathetic, and empowering guide to help you embrace your strengths and build a successful life for yourself and your children. The lessons and insights shared within these pages come from personal experience and professional expertise, ensuring you can access the most relevant and impactful information available.

This book is a companion with you as you navigate the joys and challenges of solo parenting. This book will empower you to create a nurturing and loving environment for your children, develop a strong support network, and maintain a healthy work-life balance by providing tailored solutions, resources, and support.

No longer will you feel overwhelmed, isolated, or judged – instead, you'll be equipped with the tools and confidence needed to thrive in your unique role as a single parent. So, if you're ready to take charge of your single parenting journey and raise happy, resilient children, "Single Parenting" is the perfect book for you. Let's embark on this incredible journey together and celebrate the strength, resilience, and love that define single parenthood.

Welcome to the complex and rewarding world of single parenting. This journey, while it may be sprinkled with unique challenges, is also ripe with opportunities for personal growth, resilience, and boundless love. As a single parent, you navigate a unique path, juggling multiple roles and responsibilities that require enormous strength and adaptability. This chapter aims to shed light on the realities of single parenting, helping you understand and appreciate your unique position while debunking any misconceptions or stereotypes that may surround single parenthood.

In recent years, single-parent families have become a significant part of our societal fabric, reshaping the conventional understanding of a 'nuclear family.' This evolution underscores the need for resources and guidance tailored specifically for single parents. However, before we delve into practical strategies and advice, we must have a firm grasp of the landscape of single parenthood.

What does it mean to be a single parent in today's world? What unique strengths do you bring, and what specific challenges may you encounter? Let's embark on this explorative journey together.

The Rise of Single-Parent Families

Over the past few decades, the dynamics of family structures have undergone significant transformations. One of these notable shifts is the rise of single-parent families. According to the U.S. Census Bureau, single-parent households have tripled since the 1960s. This trend is not exclusive to the United States, as similar patterns have been observed globally. The rise of single-parent families reflects several societal changes, including shifting marriage patterns, increasing divorce rates, and evolving cultural and societal norms.

The Changing Landscape of Marriage

Traditional notions of marriage have shifted considerably over the years, and more people are delaying marriage, and cohabitation before marriage has become increasingly common. This change in attitudes towards marriage has contributed to the rise in single-parent families, as more children are born out of wedlock.

Additionally, changes in societal norms and legal frameworks have made it easier for single individuals to adopt children, further contributing to the growth of single-parent households. Both men and women embrace the opportunity to parent independently, challenging the traditional idea of a two-parent family structure.

The Impact of Divorce

Another significant factor contributing to the rise of single-parent families is the increasing divorce rate. Divorce has become more socially accepted over the past few decades, and the legal process has become more accessible. As a result, more children are living in single-parent households post-divorce.

The Role of Socioeconomic Factors

Socioeconomic factors also play a crucial role in the rise of single-parent families. Economic hardships can strain marriages, leading to separation or divorce. Conversely, single parents may face financial challenges due to the high cost of raising children on a single income.

Widening Acceptance and Recognition of Single Parenthood

Over the years, society has become more accepting and understanding of single-parent families. This shift in perception has led to increased visibility and recognition of single parents in the media, popular culture, and policy discussions. The increasing acceptance has encouraged more single individuals to embrace parenthood through adoption, artificial insemination, or surrogacy.

The Influence of Technology and Modern Medicine

Advancements in reproductive technologies and modern medicine have also contributed to the rise of single-parent families. Fertility treatments, such as in-vitro fertilization (IVF) and intrauterine insemination (IUI), have enabled single individuals to conceive children without a partner. These medical advancements have empowered many single men and women to realize their dreams of becoming parents.

The Role of Support Networks

The rise of single-parent families has also led to the development of support networks and resources specifically designed to cater to the unique needs of single parents. Online communities, parenting groups, and dedicated resources have become increasingly available, providing single parents with a network of support they can rely on. This growing support system has made single parenthood more manageable and has empowered more individuals to embrace single parenting.

The rise of single-parent families is a multifaceted phenomenon influenced by various factors, including shifting societal norms, evolving family structures, increased divorce rates, advancements in reproductive technologies, and the development of support networks. As we continue our journey through this book, we must consider these factors to better understand and appreciate the unique challenges and strengths of single parenthood.

Debunking Single Parenting Myths

Several myths and misconceptions have influenced societal perspectives and attitudes toward single parenting. These misunderstandings often stem from outdated beliefs, biases, or oversimplifications, and they can unfairly stigmatize single parents and their families.

Myth 1: Single Parents Are Always "Going It Alone"

One of the most common misconceptions about single parents is that they always do it with assistance or support. The reality, however, is often quite different. Many single parents have a network of supportive family members and friends who provide emotional, practical, and sometimes financial assistance. Moreover, many single parents co-parent with their ex-partners, sharing the responsibilities and challenges of raising their children.

Myth 2: Single Parents Are Invariably Financially Strapped

While financial challenges can be part of the single parenting experience, it's not a universal truth. The financial situation of single parents can vary widely based on factors such as their employment status, income level, educational background, and the support they receive from their family or the other parent. Moreover, many single parents demonstrate incredible resourcefulness and resilience when managing their finances and providing for their families.

Myth 3: Children of Single Parents Are More Likely to Struggle Academically and Socially

Research has shown that the quality of parenting — not the number of parents — is the critical determinant of a child's academic and social success. Single parents are just as capable as coupled parents of providing the love, attention, and stability children need to thrive. Many children of single parents excel academically and socially, demonstrating resilience, independence, and adaptability.

Myth 4: Single Parents Are Always Stressed and Overwhelmed

While it's true that single parenting can bring about unique challenges and stressors, it's important to note that this doesn't mean single parents are perpetually overwhelmed. Many single parents develop impressive multitasking skills, effective time management strategies, and strong problem-solving abilities to navigate their roles efficiently. Furthermore, the sense of fulfillment and joy derived from raising a child can often outweigh the difficulties, contributing to overall resilience.

Myth 5: Single Parenting Is Always a Result of Unplanned Circumstances

Although some single parents assume this role due to unforeseen circumstances like divorce or the death of a partner, it's a myth that single parenthood is always a result of unplanned events. In recent years, there has been a rise in intentional single parenting. Advances in reproductive technology, shifting societal norms, and changing personal beliefs have made it possible for more individuals to choose to become single parents consciously.

Myth 6: Single Parents Can't Have Successful Careers

The belief that single parents can't excel professionally is a misconception. Despite the demands of single parenthood, many single parents successfully balance their parenting responsibilities with their careers. They achieve this through flexible work arrangements, quality childcare, strong support networks, and personal determination. Numerous single parents have thriving careers and are making significant contributions in their respective fields.

In debunking these myths, it's important to remember that every single parent's journey is unique. Their experiences are shaped by many factors, including their personal circumstances, resources, support networks, and individual resilience. As we delve deeper into this guide, we'll continue highlighting the diversity and complexity of single parenting experiences, challenging stereotypes, and promoting understanding.

The Unique Strengths and Challenges of Single Parenthood

Single parenthood comes with its own unique set of strengths and challenges. While demanding, it can also be gratifying and fulfilling.

The Challenges of Single Parenthood

Financial Responsibilities

One of the critical challenges single parents face is managing financial responsibilities on a single income. This includes meeting daily expenses, providing for a child's education, and saving for the future. The financial strain can be amplified by the need for quality childcare, primarily when the parent works full-time.

Time Management

Single parents often juggle multiple responsibilities, including work, childcare, household chores, and personal needs. This can make time management a significant challenge. Balancing all these demands while ensuring quality time with their children can require considerable planning and organization.

Lack of Support

Single parents may sometimes feel a lack of support, both emotionally and practically. The absence of a partner can mean fewer opportunities to share parenting responsibilities, discuss worries or concerns, or have a break. This can lead to feelings of isolation and overwhelm.

The Strengths of Single Parenthood

Despite these challenges, single parenthood also has unique strengths worth celebrating.

Independence and Self-Reliance

One of the most remarkable strengths that single parents often develop is a high degree of independence and self-reliance. Managing all aspects of family life often necessitates becoming adept at problem-solving, decision-making, and resource management.

Resilience

Single parents frequently demonstrate extraordinary resilience. The experience of overcoming difficulties and navigating challenges can lead to personal growth and a strong sense of self-efficacy.

Deep Parent-Child Bonds

Single parents often share a deep, unique bond with their children. The one-on-one time spent together can foster close relationships and mutual understanding.

Building Empathy and Understanding

Single parents often model empathy and understanding for their children. The unique circumstances of their family structure can cultivate open-mindedness and acceptance in children, equipping them to understand and navigate our diverse world better.

Developing Multi-tasking Abilities

Given the many roles single parents need to fulfill, they often become adept at multitasking. These skills can benefit various aspects of life, including work, social situations, and personal projects.

Fostering Independence in Children

Children of single parents often learn independence from a young age. They witness their parent managing various responsibilities single-handedly, which can inspire them to develop their problem-solving skills and independence.

Encouraging Teamwork

In single-parent families, it's common for older children to help with household chores or care for younger siblings. This encourages teamwork and responsibility and fosters a supportive family environment.

Nurturing a Strong Sense of Community

Single parents often seek support from their local community, neighbors, friends, or organizations. This can foster a strong sense of community and belonging for both the parent and the child.

These strengths illustrate that while single parenting can be challenging, it also offers opportunities for personal growth, resilience, and unique familial bonds. Every single parent's journey is different, shaped by individual circumstances and experiences. As we progress in this guide, we'll provide you with practical strategies and resources to leverage these strengths and navigate the challenges of single parenting.

The Varieties of Single Parenting Experiences

In the world of single parenting, there isn't a one-size-fits-all narrative. Single parenthood encompasses diverse experiences shaped by socioeconomic status, race, ethnicity, gender, and the circumstances leading to single parenthood.

Single Mothers vs. Single Fathers

Society often views single parenting through the lens of single motherhood, but it's crucial to acknowledge that single fathers constitute a significant portion of single parents. While there are commonalities in the experiences of single mothers and fathers, there are also distinct challenges and strengths associated with each.

Single Mothers

Single mothers often face societal prejudices, gender wage gaps, and expectations of fulfilling traditional caregiving roles. Despite these challenges, they frequently demonstrate resilience and strength, providing their children with nurturing environments while managing work and personal responsibilities.

Single Fathers

On the other hand, single fathers may face societal stereotypes questioning their ability to provide nurturing care. They often must navigate a world designed primarily for mothers, from parenting groups to family-friendly policies at work. However, they also continually break down gender norms, demonstrating that fathers can be just as nurturing and capable in their parenting roles.

Single Parents by Choice

The journey of single parents by choice can look different from those who become single parents due to circumstances like divorce or the death of a partner. These individuals consciously decide to parent alone, often through adoption or assisted reproductive technologies. They may face unique challenges, like societal stigma or complex processes associated with adoption or reproductive assistance. However, their experiences also underscore the changing norms of what constitutes a family as they pioneer new paths in the landscape of parenthood.

LGBTQ+ Single Parents

LGBTQ+ single parents often navigate unique challenges, from legal complexities related to parental rights to societal prejudices. However, they also contribute to the diversity and richness of single-parent families, often forging paths in non-traditional family structures and advocating for more inclusive societal norms.

As we explore these diverse experiences of single parenthood, we aim to provide a comprehensive understanding of the multifaceted world of single parenting. This understanding is the foundation for the practical advice, strategies, and tools we will provide in the upcoming chapters, tailored to single parents' diverse needs and experiences.

Stories of Resilience and Empowerment

In this section, we will share stories of resilience and empowerment from the lives of single parents. These narratives highlight single parents' strengths, struggles, and triumphs, providing inspiration and relatable experiences.

Story 1: Embracing Independence - Sarah's Story

Sarah became a single mother after her divorce. She was initially overwhelmed by the prospect of raising her two young children alone. However, Sarah took one day at a time, and slowly, she began to find her rhythm. She found strength in her independence, learning to handle all aspects of her household, from finances to repairs.

Despite her demanding schedule, Sarah ensured she spent quality time with her children, nurturing a strong bond with them. Today, Sarah manages her responsibilities efficiently and runs a successful online business, and her journey exemplifies the resilience and independence that single parents often develop.

Story 2: Shattering Stereotypes - David's Story

A single father, David faced societal stereotypes questioning his ability to raise his daughter post-divorce. Undeterred, David took on the challenge with determination. He learned to braid his daughter's hair, cooked her favorite meals, and was always there for her school events. David's story breaks the stereotype of the inept single father, showcasing that fathers can be nurturing and fully capable of caring for their children.

Story 3: Choosing Single Parenthood - Alex's Story

Alex, a successful career woman, decided in her late thirties to be a mother, even if it meant doing it alone. She adopted a baby girl and started her journey as a single parent by choice. While the adoption process was challenging, Alex says that the joy of being a parent makes it all worthwhile.

Alex's story illustrates that families can be created in many ways, and single parents, by choice, are as capable and committed as any other parents.

The world of single parenting is diverse and filled with unique experiences. It's a realm shaped by the strength, resilience, and determination of individuals who manage the challenges of raising children on their while also navigating societal norms and expectations. We've learned that single parents come from all walks of life and circumstances, each with unique stories of triumph and resilience.

These stories testify to the power of perseverance and the love single parents have for their children. These narratives not only inspire but also underscore the importance of understanding and acknowledging the varied experiences and challenges single parents face.

2. Navigating Custody Arrangements

Navigating custody arrangements is a crucial aspect of single parenting that can significantly impact the lives of both the parent and the child. The process can be emotional and challenging, involving essential decisions about the child's living arrangements, visitation schedules, and decision-making responsibilities. This chapter will explore the various types of custody, the importance of creating a well-structured parenting plan, and how to manage legal matters and court proceedings to prioritize the child's best interests.

Understanding the complexities of custody arrangements is essential for single parents, as it helps them establish a stable environment for their children while maintaining a healthy relationship with their co-parent. With clear guidelines and effective communication, single parents can create a supportive and nurturing environment for their children during this transitional period.

By thoroughly discussing the different aspects of custody arrangements, we aim to provide single parents with the knowledge and tools necessary to make informed decisions and successfully navigate the challenges of raising a child in a single-parent household.

Understanding Different Types of Custody

Navigating custody arrangements begins with understanding the various types of custody and how they may impact your family. Each custody type has its own implications for the parents and children involved.

Legal Custody

Legal custody refers to a parent's right to make significant decisions for their child, such as education, healthcare, and religious upbringing. Legal custody can be either sole or joint, depending on the circumstances.

Sole legal custody: Only one parent can make significant decisions for the child in this arrangement. This may be granted when the court determines that it is in the child's best interest for one parent to have sole decision-making power.

Joint legal custody: Joint legal custody means both parents are responsible for making important decisions for their child. This arrangement encourages cooperation and communication between parents and ensures both parties have an active role in the child's life.

Physical Custody

Physical custody pertains to where the child resides and who is responsible for their daily care. Like legal custody, physical custody can also be sole or joint.

Sole physical custody: With this arrangement, the child lives primarily with one parent responsible for daily care. The non-custodial parent may have visitation rights, which can vary in frequency and duration.

Joint physical custody: Joint physical custody, also known as shared custody, means the child spends significant time living with both parents. This arrangement requires high coordination and communication between parents to meet the child's needs.

Factors Influencing Custody Decisions

When determining custody arrangements, courts typically prioritize the child's best interests. Factors that may influence custody decisions include:

- The child's age and developmental needs

- Each parent's ability to provide a stable and nurturing environment

- The child's relationship with each parent

- The parent's ability to communicate and cooperate in matters related to the child

- The child's preference, if they are of suitable age and maturity

- Any history of domestic violence or abuse

- Each parent's work schedule and availability

Visitation Rights

In cases where one parent has sole physical custody, the non-custodial parent usually has the right to visitation, which allows them to spend time with their child. There are several types of visitation arrangements:

Unsupervised visitation is the most common type, where the non-custodial parent can spend time with the child without supervision. The visitation schedule can be flexible, with dates and times agreed upon by both parents.

Supervised visitation: In some cases, the court may require a third party to supervise the non-custodial parent's visits or take place in a designated facility. This may be necessary if there are concerns about the child's safety or the non-custodial parent's ability to provide appropriate care.

Virtual visitation: With technological advances, virtual visitation has become more common. This type of visitation involves video calls, phone calls, or other electronic means for the non-custodial parent to maintain a relationship with their child.

Modifying Custody Arrangements

Custody arrangements are sometimes flexible and may be modified if there is a significant change in circumstances. Some reasons for modification may include the following:

- Relocation of one parent

- Changes in the child's needs or circumstances

- Changes in the parents' work schedules or financial situations

- Evidence of abuse, neglect, or a detrimental environment for the child

To modify a custody arrangement, a parent must file a petition with the court and demonstrate that the change in circumstances warrants a modification. The court will then reevaluate the situation and determine if the proposed modification aligns with the child's best interests.

Temporary Custody

In some situations, a temporary custody arrangement may be implemented until a more permanent solution can be established. This could occur when there is an ongoing custody dispute, a parent's temporary inability to care for the child, or other urgent situations requiring immediate intervention. Temporary custody arrangements are subject to change and are typically reevaluated once the circumstances prompting the temporary arrangement have been resolved.

Understanding the different types of custody is a crucial aspect of navigating custody arrangements. Familiarizing yourself with the various options and their implications will help you make informed decisions and advocate for your child's best interests.

Creating a Parenting Plan

A parenting plan is a crucial tool for single parents navigating custody arrangements, as it outlines the specific agreements between parents regarding the care and upbringing of their children.

By establishing a well-thought-out parenting plan, you can create a structured and predictable environment for your child, reduce the likelihood of conflicts with your co-parent, and ensure that both parents clearly understand their roles and responsibilities.

Decision-Making Responsibilities

A well-structured parenting plan should also address decision-making responsibilities, particularly in cases where parents have joint legal custody. This includes determining how decisions will be made regarding the child's education, healthcare, religious upbringing, and other significant aspects of their life. Establishing clear guidelines for decision-making can help prevent conflicts and ensure that both parents remain involved in their child's life.

Communication Guidelines

Effective communication between co-parents is crucial for successful parenting and reducing misunderstandings. Your parenting plan should outline specific communication guidelines, such as:

- Preferred methods of communication (e.g., phone, email, text)

- Frequency of communication and updates

- Respectful communication boundaries and expectations

- How to handle disagreements or conflicts related to the parenting plan

Addressing Financial Responsibilities

Another essential aspect of a parenting plan is addressing the financial responsibilities of each parent. This may include:

- Child support payments

- Allocation of expenses for education, healthcare, and extracurricular activities

- Plans for saving for future expenses, such as college or other long-term goals

- Division of costs for childcare, transportation, and other parenting-related expenses

- Establishing clear financial expectations can help prevent disputes and ensure both parents contribute to their child's wellbeing.

Managing Legal Matters and Court Proceedings

Navigating the legal aspects of custody arrangements can be a complex and overwhelming process for single parents. Understanding your rights and responsibilities and the necessary steps to ensure the best outcome for your child is essential.

Working with a Family Law Attorney

Hiring an experienced family law attorney can make a significant difference in navigating legal matters related to custody arrangements. An attorney can help you:

- Understand your legal rights and options

- Draft or review parenting plans and custody agreements

- Represent your interests in court proceedings

- Negotiate with the other parent's attorney

- Assist with modifications to existing custody orders

When selecting an attorney, it is essential to find someone with a strong background in family law who is familiar with the specific laws and procedures in your jurisdiction. Additionally, choose an attorney who understands your goals and priorities and with whom you can communicate openly and comfortably.

Preparing for Court

If your custody case goes to court, being well-prepared can significantly impact the outcome. Here are some steps to help you prepare for court proceedings:

Gather documentation: Collect relevant documents and evidence that support your case, such as school records, medical records, and any communication between you and the other parent. Organize these documents and provide copies to your attorney.

Develop a straightforward narrative: Work with your attorney to develop a clear and concise narrative that outlines your position and demonstrates why your proposed custody arrangement is in your child's best interest.

Practice your testimony: If you are testifying in court, practice your testimony with your attorney, focusing on staying calm, clear, and composed. Be prepared to answer questions from both your attorney and the opposing party.

Dress appropriately: Presenting a professional appearance in court is crucial. Dress conservatively and ensure your clothing is clean and well-fitting.

Be punctual and respectful: Arrive early for your court date and treat everyone in the courtroom with respect, including the judge, court staff, and the opposing party.

Advocating for Your Child's Best Interests

Keeping your child's best interests at the forefront of decision-making is vital throughout the legal process. Focus on what is best for your child's emotional, physical, and mental well-being rather than getting caught up in personal conflicts with your co-parent. By maintaining a child-centered approach, you will be better equipped to advocate for an outcome that genuinely benefits your child.

Navigating Emotional Challenges During Custody Battles

Custody battles can be an emotionally challenging experience for single parents, and the stress, uncertainty, and potential conflicts can take a toll on your mental health and overall well-being. This section will explore strategies to help you navigate the emotional challenges during custody battles, providing guidance on managing stress, maintaining a support system, and prioritizing self-care.

Managing Stress and Anxiety

High levels of stress and anxiety are expected during custody battles. It is crucial to recognize the impact of stress on your health and take steps to manage it effectively. Consider implementing the following stress-management techniques:

Practice mindfulness: Engage in mindfulness exercises, such as deep breathing, meditation, or progressive muscle relaxation, to help reduce anxiety and bring your focus back to the present moment.

Exercise regularly: Physical activity can be a powerful stress reliever. Aim to engage in at least 30 minutes of moderate exercise most days of the week.

Maintain a healthy diet: Eating a balanced diet can help you feel more energized and better equipped to manage stress.

Prioritize sleep: Ensure you get sufficient sleep, as lack of rest can exacerbate stress and emotional challenges.

Set boundaries: Establish clear boundaries with your co-parent and others involved in the custody dispute to protect your emotional well-being.

Building a Support System

A robust support system can be invaluable during a custody battle. Reach out to friends, family members, and other single parents who can offer empathy, encouragement, and practical advice. Additionally, consider joining a support group specifically for single parents going through custody disputes or seeking professional help from a therapist or counselor.

Prioritizing Self-Care

Amid the emotional turmoil of a custody battle, it is essential to prioritize self-care and attend to your own emotional and physical needs. This benefits your well-being and enables you to be the best parent possible for your child. Consider the following self-care strategies:

Engage in activities you enjoy: Make time for hobbies and interests that bring you joy and help relieve stress.

Seek professional help: If you are struggling with overwhelming emotions, consider seeking help from a mental health professional, such as a therapist or counselor.

Practice self-compassion: Remind yourself that it is normal to feel a range of emotions during this challenging time, and be gentle with yourself.

Establish a daily routine: Maintaining a consistent routine can provide stability and help you feel more in control of your life.

Maintaining Effective Communication

Effective communication with your co-parent and other involved parties is essential during a custody battle. Open and respectful communication can minimize conflicts and facilitate a smoother process. Consider the following tips for maintaining effective communication:

Choose your words carefully: Be mindful of your language when discussing custody matters. Avoid using negative or accusatory language and focus on expressing your thoughts and feelings clearly and non-confrontational.

Listen actively: When your co-parent or others speak, give them your full attention and listen without interrupting. This can foster a more respectful and collaborative atmosphere.

Stay focused on the issue: Avoid bringing up unrelated issues or past conflicts during discussions about custody arrangements. Stay focused on the current topic and work toward finding a solution in your child's best interest.

Use "I" statements: When expressing your feelings and concerns, use "I" statements to avoid sounding accusatory or confrontational. For example, instead of saying, "You never help with the children," say, "I feel overwhelmed and could use more support with the children."

Keep your child's best interests at the forefront: Throughout all communication, remember that the primary goal is finding a custody arrangement in your child's best interest. This mindset can help keep conversations more productive and focused.

The Role of Mediation in Custody Arrangements

Mediation can be a valuable tool for single parents navigating custody arrangements, offering an alternative to traditional court proceedings. In this section, we will explore the benefits and process of mediation and provide tips for effectively engaging in the mediation process.

Understanding Mediation

Mediation is a voluntary, confidential, and non-adversarial process in which a neutral third-party mediator assists both parents in reaching a mutually agreeable custody arrangement. The mediator's role is to facilitate communication, encourage understanding, and help the parties explore potential solutions. Mediation can be beneficial for several reasons:

Less adversarial: Mediation encourages collaboration and problem-solving rather than pitting parents against each other, which can lead to more amicable relationships and better co-parenting outcomes.

Cost-effective: Mediation can be more affordable than traditional court proceedings, saving both parents time and money.

Customized solutions: Mediation allows parents to create a custody arrangement tailored to their family's needs and circumstances.

Confidentiality: Mediation discussions are confidential, meaning the information shared during mediation cannot be used in court.

Control: Mediation enables parents to control the decision-making process rather than having a judge determine the outcome.

Tips for Effective Mediation

To make the most of the mediation process, consider the following tips:

Choose the right mediator: Select a mediator with experience in family law and child custody issues and a communication style that aligns with your preferences.

Prepare in advance: Gather relevant documentation and information, such as work schedules, school calendars, and financial records, to help inform the mediation discussions.

Be open to compromise: Mediation requires both parties to compromise and consider alternative solutions. Approach the process with an open mind and a commitment to finding a resolution in your child's best interest.

Prioritize your child's needs: Keep your child's well-being and best interests at the forefront of all discussions and decision-making.

Communicate effectively: Practice active listening, express yourself clearly, and stay focused on the issue at hand during mediation sessions.

3. Co-Parenting Dynamics

Welcome to Chapter 3, where we delve into the intricate dynamics of co-parenting. As a single parent, understanding co-parenting dynamics is crucial to maintaining a healthy relationship with your child and their other parent. Co-parenting is a shared responsibility that demands mutual respect, communication, and compromise. It may seem daunting, especially after a separation or divorce. Still, it can be a positive and productive journey for everyone involved with the right strategies and mindset.

This chapter will equip you with practical and effective strategies to navigate the often-complex world of co-parenting. We will explore establishing healthy boundaries, improving communication, and constructively addressing conflicts and disagreements.

By the end of this chapter, you will be better prepared to face the challenges and rewards that come with co-parenting and create an environment that prioritizes your child's well-being. This is not just about managing the relationship with your co-parent but ensuring that your child grows up in a nurturing and supportive environment, regardless of the family structure.

Establishing Healthy Boundaries

The establishment of healthy boundaries serves as the cornerstone of effective co-parenting. Boundaries not only shape the nature of your interaction with your co-parent but also set the stage for a stable and harmonious environment for your child. Establishing clear and firm boundaries reduces confusion, helps manage expectations, and significantly lowers the potential for conflicts.

Understanding the Concept of Boundaries in Co-parenting

Boundaries in co-parenting refer to the precise definition and understanding of each parent's roles, responsibilities, and personal space. They provide a framework for interaction and serve as a guide for what is acceptable and what is not in your relationship with your co-parent. It's crucial to note that these boundaries are not designed to create a divide or promote isolation. Instead, they foster mutual respect and develop a sense of safety and predictability for all parties involved, particularly for the child.

Why Boundaries Are Important

Boundaries in co-parenting are essential for multiple reasons. Firstly, they establish a clear division of responsibilities, ensuring parents understand their individual and joint tasks in raising their child. Secondly, boundaries help manage expectations and reduce the chances of misunderstandings that can lead to disagreements or conflicts. Lastly, boundaries help protect the child's emotional well-being. Children thrive in environments with consistency and structure, and setting and respecting boundaries provides a secure and predictable environment for your child to grow and develop.

Steps to Establish Healthy Boundaries

Establishing healthy boundaries in co-parenting involves several steps. It begins with a candid discussion with your co-parent about your expectations, concerns, and hopes for your shared parenting journey. This conversation should be respectful and open, allowing both parties to express their thoughts freely.

After this discussion, you can start to outline the specific boundaries. These include who cares for the child during particular days, how decisions about the child's education and health are made, and guidelines for introducing new partners. Remember that these boundaries should be flexible and subject to review and adjustment as your child grows and circumstances change.

Respecting and Maintaining Boundaries

Once the boundaries are established, the next step is ensuring they are respected and maintained. This might require frequent communication and check-ins with your co-parent. In some situations, it may be beneficial to involve a neutral third party, such as a counselor or mediator, to assist in maintaining these boundaries.

Remember, establishing healthy boundaries in co-parenting is a continuous process that requires patience, understanding, and mutual respect. It's not about winning or losing but about creating the best possible environment for your child to thrive. Setting clear and respectful boundaries lays the foundation for a successful co-parenting relationship.

Communication Strategies for Effective Co-Parenting

Good communication is the cornerstone of successful co-parenting, and it's the key to managing shared responsibilities, resolving conflicts, and ensuring the well-being of your children. However, communicating effectively can be challenging, especially after a separation or divorce.

Understanding the Importance of Effective Communication

Understanding why communication is vital in co-parenting is the first step in improving your strategies. Good communication helps to eliminate misunderstandings and reduce conflicts. Making shared decisions about your children's education, health, and social activities is crucial. It also provides a platform for parents to discuss and resolve any issues that may impact their children's emotional and psychological well-being.

Fostering Open and Honest Dialogue

Open and honest dialogue is fundamental to successful co-parenting. It is essential to create a safe space where both parents feel comfortable expressing their thoughts, feelings, and concerns about their children's welfare. This involves being transparent about your intentions and expectations and actively listening to your co-parent. It's not about winning an argument but about finding common ground for the best interest of your children.

Implementing a Structured Communication Plan

Having a structured communication plan can significantly improve the co-parenting process. This could involve setting regular times for discussions, deciding on the best methods of communication (be it through phone calls, emails, or in-person meetings), and agreeing on how to handle emergencies. A structured plan can minimize miscommunication, ensure both parents are up-to-date with relevant information, and reduce unnecessary contact that could lead to conflicts.

Using Neutral Language and Tone

The way you communicate is just as important as what you share. Using neutral language and tone can prevent conversations from escalating into arguments. It's essential to focus on the issue and avoid bringing up past disputes. Try to express your thoughts calmly and respectfully and avoid blaming or criticizing your co-parent. Remember, your primary goal is to create a harmonious environment for your children.

Maintaining Consistent Messages

Consistency is vital in co-parenting communication. Sending mixed messages can confuse children and create instability in their lives. Ensure that you and your co-parent are on the same page regarding rules, discipline, and values. This creates a predictable environment for your children and reduces the potential for manipulation or playing one parent against another.

Using Technology to Facilitate Communication

Technology can be a valuable tool for co-parenting communication in today's digital age. Numerous apps and online platforms are designed to help co-parents manage shared schedules, track expenses, and exchange information about their children. These tools can streamline communication, reduce the chance of misunderstandings, and provide a written record of agreements and discussions.

Prioritizing the Child's Perspective

Keeping the child's perspective at the forefront is essential in all communication. Often, parents can become so embroiled in their feelings toward each other that they overlook how their words and actions might impact the child. Children are incredibly perceptive, and parental conflict can create a stressful environment that hinders their development and well-being.

To prioritize the child's perspective, aim to separate your personal feelings about your ex-partner from your co-parenting responsibilities. This is easier said than done, but it's vital for maintaining a healthy co-parenting relationship. Remember, conversations should focus on your child's needs and best interests, not your grievances.

Practicing Active Listening

Active listening is a crucial component of effective communication, and it involves fully concentrating, understanding, responding, and then remembering what is being said. This might seem straightforward, but it's surprisingly easy to let your mind wander during conversations, mainly when the topic is sensitive or you feel defensive.

Active listening is essential in co-parenting situations, where understanding each other's perspectives can lead to better cooperation. When your co-parent is speaking, try to remain fully present and focused. Please resist interrupting or formulating your response while they're still talking. Show that you're engaged with what they're saying by nodding or giving verbal affirmations like "I see" or "I understand." This not only shows respect but also encourages open and honest communication.

Being Clear and Concise

Clarity and conciseness are essential in co-parenting communication. Beating around the bush or using vague language can lead to misunderstandings and frustration. Be as clear and direct as possible when discussing issues or making requests. State your concerns honestly but respectfully, and specify what you need from your co-parent.

For instance, instead of saying, "You never help with the schoolwork," you could say, "I've noticed that I've been handling most of the schoolwork recently. Could we discuss a more balanced division of this responsibility?" The latter is more evident, more specific, and less likely to put your co-parent on the defensive.

Considering Professional Mediation

In some cases, despite your best efforts, you and your co-parent might still need help to communicate effectively. This is where professional mediation can be beneficial. A trained mediator can facilitate discussions, help you resolve disputes, and guide you toward a mutually beneficial agreement. While this is an additional expense, it can be a worthwhile investment for peace of mind and improved co-parenting relationship.

Addressing Conflict and Disagreements

Conflict is an inevitable part of any relationship, and co-parenting is no exception. Differences in parenting styles, unresolved emotional issues, and communication breakdowns can all lead to disagreements. However, how you handle these conflicts can significantly impact your children's emotional health and your co-parenting relationship.

Recognizing the Root Causes of Conflict

Before you can effectively address conflict, it's crucial to understand its root causes. Conflicts in co-parenting often stem from unresolved emotional issues from the relationship, differing parenting styles and values, or feelings of unfairness in the division of parenting duties. Recognizing the source of your disagreements can provide insight into how to approach resolution and prevent similar conflicts in the future.

Developing a Conflict Resolution Plan

Having a predefined conflict resolution plan can be a game-changer in handling disagreements. This can involve setting rules for engagement, like agreeing to take a time-out when discussions become heated or deciding to discuss contentious issues at a neutral location. A conflict resolution plan also includes steps to take if you can't resolve a conflict independently, such as involving a mediator or counselor.

Using I-Statements for Constructive Communication

When discussing a disagreement, it's easy to fall into the trap of blaming or criticizing the other parent, and this can quickly escalate conflict and shut down effective communication. Instead, try to use I-statements that focus on your feelings and needs rather than attacking the other person. For instance, instead of saying, "You're always late for pickups," you could say, "I feel stressed when I'm uncertain about pickup times. Could we discuss a way to make this more consistent?"

Emphasizing Respect and Empathy

Respect and empathy are essential to effective conflict resolution. This means treating the other parent as an equal partner in raising your children, even if you disagree. Try to understand their point of view and validate their feelings, even if you disagree. This can help to de-escalate conflict and pave the way for a more constructive conversation.

Focusing on the Best Interest of the Child

Keeping your child's best interest at the forefront is essential in all disagreements. This can help you and your co-parent move past personal differences and focus on finding solutions that best meet your child's needs. Remember, the goal is not to "win" the argument but to create the best possible environment for your child.

Seeking Professional Help

Sometimes, despite your best efforts, conflicts can become too complex or emotionally charged to handle alone. In these cases, it can be helpful to seek professional help. Therapists, counselors, or mediators specializing in co-parenting can provide guidance, facilitate effective communication, and help you and your co-parent develop strategies for resolving future disagreements. This is not a sign of failure but a proactive step towards creating a more harmonious co-parenting relationship.

Keeping the Big Picture in Mind

Lastly, losing sight of the bigger picture in the heat of conflict is easy. While disagreements are part of the co-parenting journey, it's important to remember that you and your co-parent share a common goal: to raise happy, healthy, and well-adjusted children. Focusing on this shared objective allows you to navigate conflicts more effectively and build a stronger co-parenting partnership.

Navigating Legal and Financial Discussions

Co-parenting often involves navigating complex legal and financial discussions, which can significantly impact your lives and your children's well-being. These conversations may involve child support, custody agreements, education expenses, healthcare, and other related topics. Despite the complexities, it's vital to approach these discussions with clarity, respect, and a focus on your child's best interests.

Understanding Legal Obligations

To navigate legal discussions effectively, it's crucial to understand your legal obligations as a co-parent clearly. This includes knowing your rights and responsibilities under your custody agreement, child support obligations, and other legal directives. You may need to consult with a family law attorney to ensure you fully understand these aspects.

Maintaining Open and Honest Communication

Honesty is critical when discussing financial and legal matters. This means being transparent about your financial situation, which can impact child support and other shared expenses. It also means being open about changes in your circumstances that might affect your co-parenting arrangement. Maintaining this level of openness can build trust and prevent misunderstandings or conflicts.

Creating a Co-Parenting Budget

Creating a co-parenting budget can be a helpful tool in managing shared expenses. This budget should include regular child support payments and variable expenses like healthcare, education, and extracurricular activities. By outlining these costs, you can ensure that both parents contribute pretty and that all financial expectations are clear.

Planning for the Future

Future planning is an often overlooked but crucial part of financial discussions. This includes planning for your child's long-term needs, such as education, healthcare, and retirement. Discussing these topics early and updating your plans as necessary is essential.

Handling Disagreements Respectfully

Disagreements over financial and legal matters are common in co-parenting, but it's essential to handle these conflicts respectfully. This might involve taking a break when discussions become heated, using I-statements to express your feelings, or even involving a mediator to facilitate a resolution. Remember, the goal is to find a solution in your child's best interests, not to win the argument.

Seeking Professional Advice

Given the complexities of legal and financial discussions, it's often beneficial to seek professional advice. A family law attorney can provide legal guidance, while a financial planner can help you manage shared expenses and plan for the future. These professionals can provide objective advice and help you make informed decisions.

Setting Clear Boundaries

In financial and legal discussions, setting clear boundaries is critical. These boundaries help define each parent's responsibilities and rights, preventing conflicts or misunderstandings. For instance, if one parent is responsible for health insurance and the other for educational costs, this should be clearly outlined and agreed upon. Setting boundaries also applies to the level of financial information you're willing to share and the methods through which you're comfortable discussing these sensitive topics.

Dealing with Non-Compliance

There may be instances where one parent fails to meet their legal or financial obligations. This could be failing to pay child support on time, not sticking to the agreed-upon visitation schedule, or not contributing to shared expenses. In these situations, it's essential to address the issue directly and assertively, emphasizing the impact of non-compliance on the child. If non-compliance continues, seeking legal advice or involving a mediator might be necessary.

Adjusting Agreements Over Time

It's essential to understand that your financial and legal agreements may need to change over time. As your child grows, their needs and expenses will change. Similarly, changes in your or your co-parent's financial situation may require adjustments to child support or other financial arrangements. Regularly reviewing and updating your agreements can ensure they remain fair and meet your child's evolving needs.

Keeping Records

Keeping thorough records of all financial transactions related to your child can provide clarity and prevent disputes. This includes keeping track of child support payments, shared expenses, and any financial agreements you make. These records can serve as evidence if there's a disagreement or if you need to demonstrate your financial contributions in a legal setting.

Prioritizing Emotional Well-being

While handling legal and financial matters effectively is crucial, it's equally important not to let these discussions overshadow your child's emotional well-being. Engaging in heated arguments about money or legal issues in front of your child can cause them stress and anxiety. Try to keep these discussions separate from your interactions with your child and reassure them that both parents are working together to care for their needs.

Navigating legal and financial discussions as a co-parent can be challenging. Still, creating a fair and effective plan with open communication, mutual respect, and a focus on your child's needs is possible. Remember, it's okay to seek help when needed, whether from a financial advisor, attorney, or mediator. The ultimate goal is to ensure that your child feels secure and loved, regardless of the financial or legal arrangements between the parents.

Co-Parenting with an Uncooperative Ex-Partner

Co-parenting isn't always smooth sailing, and sometimes you might find yourself trying to establish a healthy co-parenting relationship with an ex-partner who is uncooperative or challenging to deal with. These situations can be emotionally taxing and might leave you frustrated or overwhelmed. However, some strategies can help you navigate these circumstances effectively.

Staying Focused on the Child

In situations where the other parent is being difficult, focusing on what matters most is your child's well-being is essential. This means setting aside personal differences and making decisions based on what's best for your child, not based on what might inconvenience or annoy your ex-partner. Remember, your child's emotional health, stability, and happiness should always be your top priority.

Practicing Emotional Detachment

When dealing with an uncooperative ex-partner, practicing emotional detachment is crucial; this means not letting your ex's actions or words impact your emotions or responses. By keeping your emotions in check, you can respond more effectively and avoid escalating the situation.

Effective Communication Techniques

Effective communication is critical when dealing with an uncooperative ex-partner. This might involve using neutral language, focusing on facts rather than feelings, and clearly expressing your needs and expectations. Even if your ex-partner does not communicate effectively, maintaining your communication standards can help mitigate conflict.

Seeking Professional Support

When co-parenting with an uncooperative ex-partner, professional support can be invaluable. This could include a family therapist who can provide strategies for managing conflict and improving communication. This parenting coordinator can help you navigate co-parenting logistics or a legal professional who can protect your rights and your child's interests.

Maintaining Consistency for Your Child

When one parent is uncooperative, maintaining a consistent routine for your child can provide them with stability and security. This means keeping regular schedules for meals, homework, bedtime, and other activities, regardless of what's happening between you and your ex. Consistency helps your child know what to expect, which can be exceptionally comforting in times of change or conflict.

Managing Negative Feelings

Co-parenting with an uncooperative ex can bring up various negative feelings, including anger, frustration, or sadness. Acknowledging these feelings and finding healthy ways to manage them is essential. This could involve talking with a trusted friend or therapist, engaging in stress-relieving activities, or practicing mindfulness. Taking care of your emotional well-being is crucial, not just for your own sake but also for your ability to parent effectively.

Resolving Disputes

Despite your best efforts, disputes may arise when co-parenting with an uncooperative ex. When they do, it's essential to approach them calmly and constructively. Try to understand your ex's perspective and find common ground where possible. If disputes continue, involving a neutral third party, such as a mediator or legal professional, might help resolve the issue.

Staying Positive

Even in the face of uncooperative behavior from your ex, try to stay positive, both for your sake and your child's. Remember that your ex's actions do not define your experience as a parent. You can create a nurturing, loving environment for your child, regardless of your ex's behavior. This might involve focusing on the good aspects of your life, maintaining a solid support network, and celebrating your successes as a single parent.

Co-parenting with an uncooperative ex-partner can be challenging, but with the right strategies and a child-focused perspective, you can navigate this path effectively. Remember that you're not alone; don't hesitate to seek support when needed. Your resilience and dedication make you a fantastic parent, and they will carry you through even the toughest co-parenting challenges.

Navigating the world of co-parenting, particularly with an uncooperative ex-partner, is a journey filled with challenges. However, you can successfully maneuver these turbulent waters by keeping your child's well-being as the central focus, practicing emotional detachment, maintaining effective communication, and seeking professional help.

4. Financial Management for Single Parents

Money matters can often seem overwhelming, particularly when you're managing them on your own. The financial challenges single parents face are unique and can sometimes feel insurmountable. In this pivotal chapter, we aim to alleviate some of the anxiety and uncertainty surrounding these issues by presenting clear, actionable strategies to help single parents take control of their financial situation. We will tackle everything from budgeting and saving tips to understanding taxes as a single parent, providing you with a comprehensive financial toolkit for the solo parenting journey.

Budgeting and Saving Tips

Navigating the world of finances as a single parent can seem daunting, but with the right tools and strategies, it's a challenge you can conquer. Budgeting and saving play a critical role in financial stability and are fundamental skills to master.

Understanding Your Financial Situation

Before you can begin to budget effectively, it's vital to have a clear understanding of your current financial situation. This involves:

Tracking your income: List all your sources of income, including your salary, child support, alimony, and any government benefits or assistance you receive.

Identifying your expenses: Track your spending for a few weeks to a month to get an accurate picture of where your money goes. Categorize these expenses into needs (rent, groceries, utilities, etc.) and wants (eating out, entertainment, etc.).

Creating a Budget

You can begin crafting a budget once you've got a handle on your income and expenses. Here are the key steps:

Prioritize your needs: Ensure your budget covers the essential expenses first – these are your rent or mortgage, utilities, groceries, and transportation costs. Include any fixed payments such as loans or credit card debts.

Allocate for wants: After covering your needs, allocate a portion of your income to non-essential expenses. This will provide some flexibility and enjoyment, making your budget more sustainable.

Include savings: Aim to save a percentage of your income each month. Even small amounts add up over time and can be invaluable during an emergency.

Plan for unexpected expenses: Set aside a small amount each month to cover unexpected costs such as car repairs or medical expenses.

Saving Tips for Single Parents

Saving on a single income can be challenging, but it's not impossible. Here are some effective saving strategies:

Automate your savings: Set up automatic transfers to your account each payday. This "out of sight, out of mind" approach can make saving more effortless.

Trim non-essential spending: Review your expenses and identify areas where you can cut back. This might involve eating out less, canceling unused subscriptions, or switching to a cheaper cell phone plan.

Shop smarter: Use coupons, shop sales, buy in bulk, or consider second-hand for specific items to save money.

Teach your children about money: It's always early enough to start teaching your children about the value of money. Please encourage them to save their allowances and involve them in budgeting decisions where appropriate. This eases some pressure off you and equips them with valuable life skills.

Remember, it's okay if your budget could be better right away. Budgeting is a skill that takes time to master. Be patient with yourself and adjust your budget as needed. The important part is that you're taking proactive steps toward a more secure financial future. In the next section, we will delve into the complex world of child support and alimony, guiding how to navigate these economic areas as a single parent.

Navigating Child Support and Alimony

Child support and alimony can be significant financial considerations for single parents. Understanding the legalities and responsibilities related to these payments is vital to maintain financial stability and ensuring your children's well-being.

Understanding Child Support

Child support is a legal obligation paid by the non-custodial parent to the custodial parent to assist in covering the costs associated with raising a child. Child support ensures that the child's living standards are maintained and their needs met, even when parents live separately. The courts typically determine the amount of child support and depend on various factors such as the income of both parents, the number of children, and the child's specific needs.

Some essential aspects to keep in mind regarding child support are:

Consistency: Child support should be paid consistently and on time. Failure to do so can lead to legal consequences.

Use: Child support is meant to cover a child's essential needs, including food, shelter, clothing, medical care, and educational expenses.

Legal Help: Legal action may be necessary if the non-custodial parent does not meet child support obligations. A family law attorney can provide guidance and support in such situations.

Understanding Alimony

Alimony, also known as spousal support, is a financial obligation paid by one ex-spouse to the other after divorce or separation. Unlike child support, alimony is designed to limit any unfair economic impacts of a divorce by providing ongoing income to the lower-wage-earning or non-wage-earning spouse.

Key points to remember about alimony include:

Determination: The amount and duration of alimony are determined by various factors, including the length of the marriage, each spouse's earning capacity, the standard of living established during the marriage, and the age and health of each spouse.

Changes: Alimony can be modified or terminated if circumstances change significantly, such as the receiving spouse getting remarried or the paying spouse experiencing a significant reduction in income.

Legal Advice: A lawyer can provide valuable advice and assistance when negotiating or modifying alimony agreements.

Both child support and alimony can significantly impact your financial situation as a single parent. Seeking legal advice if you need clarification or circumstances change is vital. In the following section, we will explore various financial assistance and resources available to single parents, providing you with information on how to access these valuable forms of support.

Financial Assistance and Resources for Single Parents

As a single parent, you may face financial challenges in providing for your family. Awareness of the various financial assistance programs and resources available to help support you and your children is crucial.

Government Assistance Programs

Numerous government assistance programs are designed to help single parents and low-income families. These programs can provide valuable financial support and resources to ensure the well-being of your family. Some of the most common programs include:

Temporary Assistance for Needy Families (TANF): This program provides cash assistance and support services to low-income families with children.

Supplemental Nutrition Assistance Program (SNAP): Also known as food stamps, SNAP offers financial assistance to low-income individuals and families to help them purchase food.

Medicaid: This state and federal program provides health insurance coverage to low-income individuals and families.

Children's Health Insurance Program (CHIP): CHIP offers low-cost health insurance for children in families who earn too much to qualify for Medicaid but cannot afford private health insurance.

Educational Assistance

Education is vital for your child's future success. As a single parent, you may need financial assistance to cover educational expenses such as tuition, books, and supplies. Some educational assistance options include:

Federal Pell Grants: These grants provide financial assistance to undergraduate students based on financial need.

Scholarships: Various organizations offer scholarships to students based on factors such as academic achievement, community involvement, and financial need. You can search for scholarships through online databases or contact local schools and community organizations.

Tuition assistance programs: Some employers and labor unions offer tuition assistance programs to help cover education costs for employees and their children.

Housing Assistance

Housing can be a significant expense for single parents. Fortunately, housing assistance programs are available to help you secure safe and affordable housing for your family. Some options include:

Public Housing: This government-funded program provides affordable rental housing to low-income families, elderly individuals, and persons with disabilities.

Section 8 Housing Choice Voucher Program: This program offers financial assistance to eligible families to help them rent privately-owned housing units.

Low-Income Home Energy Assistance Program (LIHEAP): This program provides financial assistance to low-income households to help them cover their energy bills.

Local Community Resources

In addition to government programs, you may find financial assistance and resources through local community organizations, such as:

Food banks and pantries: These organizations provide free or low-cost food to needy families.

Childcare assistance programs: Some community organizations offer subsidies or sliding-scale fees to help cover childcare costs for low-income families.

Nonprofit organizations: Local nonprofit organizations may offer various forms of financial assistance and support services for single parents, such as counseling, job training, and emergency assistance.

By being proactive and taking advantage of the various financial assistance programs and resources available, you can help ensure that you and your children can access the support you need. In the next section, we will discuss understanding taxes as a single parent, providing you with the information necessary to navigate the tax system and make the most of the tax benefits available.

Understanding Taxes as a Single Parent

Taxes can be a complex and intimidating aspect of personal finance, especially for single parents who must navigate them alone. However, understanding how taxes work and the available tax benefits can provide substantial financial relief and additional resources for you and your children.

Filing Status

The first thing to understand is your filing status, which significantly impacts your tax liability and eligibility for certain tax benefits. As a single parent, the two most relevant filing statuses are 'Single' and 'Head of Household.'

Single: This status is for individuals who are unmarried, divorced, or legally separated as of the last day of the tax year.

Head of Household: If you are unmarried and have provided more than half the cost of keeping up a home for yourself and a qualifying person (typically your child or dependent) for more than half the tax year, you may be eligible to file as Head of Household. This status offers more favorable tax rates and a higher standard deduction than the 'Single' filing status.

Tax Credits and Deductions

Several tax credits and deductions can significantly reduce your tax bill, and some can even result in a refund. The most important ones for single parents include:

Earned Income Tax Credit (EITC): This refundable tax credit is designed for low to moderate-income working individuals and families. The amount of the credit varies depending on your income level and the number of qualifying children you have.

Child Tax Credit: This credit is available for parents of children under 17. The amount of the credit depends on your income level and the number of eligible children you have.

Child and Dependent Care Credit: If you pay for childcare for a child under 13 so that you can work or look for work, you may qualify for this credit. The credit is a percentage of the amount you paid for childcare, with the rate depending on your income.

Dependent Exemption: Although personal and dependent exemptions were eliminated with the Tax Cuts and Jobs Act of 2017, they are still relevant for state taxes in some cases.

Child Support and Alimony

In general, child support payments are not deductible by the payer and are not taxable to the recipient. On the other hand, alimony payments are no longer deductible by the payer or considered income for the recipient for divorce or separation agreements executed after December 31, 2018.

Understanding your tax obligations and the available credits and deductions is critical to minimizing your tax liability and maximizing your refund. When in doubt, consulting with a tax professional who can guide you through the process and ensure you claim all the benefits you're entitled to can be beneficial.

5. Balancing Work and Family Life

As a single parent, balancing work and family life is one of the most significant challenges you face. You are your child's sole provider and primary caregiver, and juggling these two demanding roles can sometimes feel overwhelming. On the one hand, you must ensure you're fulfilling your professional duties to provide for your family financially. Conversely, you want to ensure you're present and engaged in your children's lives, meeting their emotional, physical, and developmental needs. This chapter aims to provide practical strategies and resources to help you successfully balance these dual roles and minimize stress in your daily life.

This chapter will explore various aspects of managing work and family life as a single parent. We will delve into time management strategies that can help you optimize your daily routines and discuss flexible work options that better suit your unique circumstances. We'll also touch on the importance of building a robust support network and provide tips for nurturing your career growth while maintaining a healthy family life.

Time Management Strategies

Effective time management is one of the critical aspects of balancing work and family life as a single parent. With only 24 hours a day, it's essential to optimize your time to ensure that your professional responsibilities and your family's needs are met.

The first step in effective time management is creating a structured routine. A predictable schedule can help provide a sense of security and stability for your children, and it can also help you stay organized and prevent essential tasks from falling through the cracks. Start by identifying your family's needs and priorities, such as work hours, school schedules, extracurricular activities, mealtimes, and bedtimes. Once you have these foundational elements, you can build your routine.

Here are some strategies to help you effectively manage your time:

Prioritize tasks: Only some things on your to-do list are equally important.

Learn to prioritize your tasks based on their urgency and importance. This can help you focus on what matters and avoid wasting time on less significant tasks.

Delegate: Remember, you don't have to do everything yourself. Delegate tasks where possible. Depending on their age and capabilities, your children can take on specific responsibilities, such as tidying their rooms or helping with chores. This can free up some time and teach your children essential life skills.

Utilize technology: Numerous apps and tools can help you manage your time more effectively. Technology can be a great ally in your time management efforts, from calendar apps that keep track of appointments and deadlines to meal planning apps that simplify grocery shopping and cooking.

Learn to say no: It's essential to understand that there are limits to what you can achieve in a day. Be bold and avoid additional responsibilities that could overwhelm you or disrupt your work-life balance.

Make time for self-care: While it might seem counter-intuitive when discussing time management, setting aside time for self-care is crucial. Remember, you can't pour from an empty cup. Taking care of your physical and mental health can make you more productive and resilient in the long run.

Effective time management is not about packing as many tasks as possible into your day. It's about simplifying how you work, getting things done faster, and freeing up time so you can enjoy your life and your children more. It's about creating a balance that helps you feel less stressed and more in control and allows you to be your best parent.

Flexible Work Options for Single Parents

In today's fast-paced world, the traditional 9-to-5 work schedule might only be feasible for some single parents. Balancing work, family responsibilities, and personal time can be a challenge, especially when you're the sole caregiver for your children. Thankfully, many employers are recognizing the need for more flexible work arrangements.

Remote Work: With technological advancements, remote work has become increasingly popular and accessible across various industries. This option allows you to work from home, eliminating commuting time and offering more flexibility to manage home responsibilities alongside work tasks. However, creating boundaries between work and personal life is crucial to avoid burnout.

Flexible Hours: Some employers may allow you to adjust your working hours to align with your obligations better. This could mean starting and ending your workday earlier or later than the traditional schedule or working longer but fewer days a week.

Part-time Work: If you can afford fewer hours, part-time work can be a good option. This can give you more time during the day to spend with your children and manage household duties.

Job Sharing: Job sharing involves splitting a full-time position with another employee. You share the responsibilities of one job, and this can allow for more flexibility in your schedule.

Freelance or Contract Work: Freelance or contract work can offer a high degree of flexibility, as you often have control over your schedule and the projects you take on. However, it's worth noting that these roles may offer additional job security or benefits than traditional employment.

Remember, the best flexible work option for you will depend on your unique circumstances and needs, including your financial situation, your child's age and care needs, and your personal career goals. It's also important to communicate openly with your employer about your needs and challenges as a single parent. Many companies have policies to support working parents and may be willing to accommodate flexible work arrangements.

Building a Support Network

No one is an island, which is especially true for single parents. The truth is, you can't do it all alone, nor should you have to. A reliable and supportive network of friends, family, and community members can make a difference in your parenting journey. A strong support network can provide emotional support, practical help, and much-needed respite from your responsibilities. Here, we'll explore strategies to build and strengthen your support network.

Reaching out to Friends and Family: The first step to building your support network is reaching out to the people closest to you—your friends and family. They can provide emotional support, help with childcare, and even assistance with grocery shopping or home repairs. Don't be afraid to ask for help when you need it. Often, your loved ones will be more than willing to lend a hand.

Connecting with Other Single Parents: Who can understand the unique challenges of single parenthood better than other single parents? Look for local or online single-parent support groups where you can share experiences, advice, and resources. These groups can provide a sense of community and understanding that is hard to find elsewhere.

Utilizing Community Resources: Your community can be a valuable source of support. Look for local resources such as parenting classes, community centers, and religious organizations that support single parents. Many communities also have resources like food banks and clothing drives that can provide practical help.

Building Relationships with Teachers and Caregivers: Teachers, babysitters, and other caregivers play a significant role in your child's life. Building solid relationships with them can ensure your child gets the best possible care and can also provide you with additional support and understanding.

Online Support: Online communities and forums can provide round-the-clock support and a wealth of resources. Websites, blogs, and social media groups dedicated to single parenting can provide advice, share experiences, and offer emotional support to people in the same boat worldwide.

Remember, it's okay to lean on others for support. Everyone needs help sometimes, and you're doing the best you can. By building a solid support network, you're helping yourself and providing your child with a community of people who care about their well-being.

Managing Career Growth as a Single Parent

Being a single parent doesn't mean you have to put your career aspirations on hold. Pursuing your career can provide financial security for your family and serve as a powerful example for your children about the value of hard work, perseverance, and ambition. However, managing career growth as a single parent requires strategic planning and careful consideration.

Set Clear Career Goals: The first step in managing your career growth is clearly understanding your goals. What do you want to achieve in your career, and what steps do you need to take to get there? Clear career goals can guide your decision-making and help you prioritize your efforts.

Develop a Career Plan: Once you have clear career goals, create a plan to achieve them. This could include further education or training, seeking mentorship in your field, or taking on new responsibilities at work. A well-thought-out career plan can help you navigate your career path more effectively and make decisions that align with your long-term goals.

Seek Work-Life Balance: Striving for career success doesn't mean neglecting family responsibilities. It's crucial to seek a balance between your work and home life. This might involve negotiating flexible work hours, working from home, or using childcare services. Remember, achieving work-life balance is about time management and ensuring you have time to rest and recharge.

Networking: Building professional relationships is vital for career growth. Networking can open up opportunities for mentorship, collaboration, and job opportunities. Attend industry events, join professional organizations, and connect with colleagues on networking sites like LinkedIn.

Continuing Education and Training: In many fields, continuing education and training can be vital to advancing your career. Look for opportunities to expand your skills and knowledge through formal education, online courses, professional development workshops, or industry certifications.

Self-Care and Resilience: Balancing career growth with single parenthood can be challenging, and it's essential to prioritize self-care and build resilience. This includes maintaining a healthy lifestyle, seeking support, and practicing stress management techniques. Remember, taking care of yourself is not a luxury but a necessity for you and your family.

Navigating career growth as a single parent may not always be easy, but it's certainly possible with determination, planning, and the proper support. By setting clear goals, creating a career plan, and maintaining a healthy work-life balance, you can continue to advance your career while providing for your family.

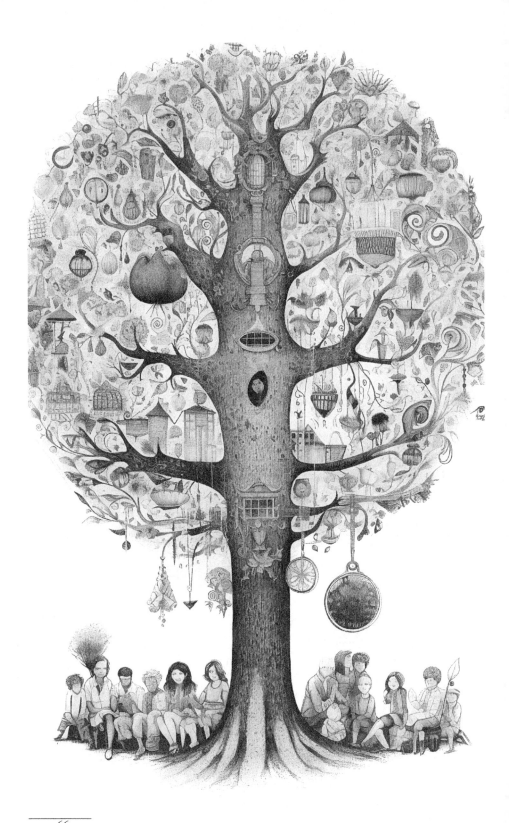

6. Parenting Techniques for Single Parents

Single parents want to raise their children to be happy, healthy, and well-adjusted like all parents. This is no small task, and the responsibility can feel even more significant when handling it alone. However, equipped with the right tools and strategies, single parents can effectively guide their children's development and instill the values and skills needed for success in life.

This chapter will explore several essential parenting techniques tailored specifically for single parents. From positive discipline and behavior management strategies to fostering emotional resilience, creating a nurturing home environment, promoting social skills, and teaching respect and values, this chapter offers a comprehensive guide to effective single parenting. Let's embark on this journey together, knowing we can raise our children to thrive in today's complex world with patience, empathy, and understanding.

Positive Discipline and Behavior Management

The foundation of effective parenting is rooted in the strategies used to guide children's behavior and discipline them when necessary. As a single parent, it is essential to establish a system that promotes positive behavior and discourages negative actions.

Positive discipline is a respectful and encouraging method of guiding children's behavior. Unlike punitive discipline methods that rely on fear or punishment, positive discipline focuses on teaching children the reasoning behind rules and encouraging them to make better choices. This approach not only promotes better behavior in the short term but also helps children develop critical thinking skills, empathy, and a sense of responsibility.

Here are some strategies for implementing positive discipline:

Set clear and consistent rules: Children thrive on structure and consistency. Clearly outline your expectations and the consequences of not meeting them. Consistency in enforcing these rules is critical.

Use natural and logical consequences: Rather than imposing arbitrary punishments, let your children experience the natural outcomes of their actions. For instance, if a child refuses to do their homework, the natural consequence could be a poor grade.

Validate their feelings: Acknowledge your child's feelings before addressing the behavior, and this validation helps them feel understood and more open to hearing your perspective.

Problem-solving together: Work with your child to find a mutually satisfying solution when conflicts arise. This collaborative approach promotes empathy and problem-solving skills.

Model the behavior you expect: Children learn by example. Display the behaviors you want your child to emulate, such as respect, honesty, and kindness.

Reinforce positive behavior: Always remember to acknowledge and reward good behavior. Positive reinforcement can come in many forms, such as praise, additional privileges, or small rewards, which will motivate your child to repeat the behavior in the future.

Communicate effectively: Communicate your expectations clearly and listen attentively to your child's perspective. Open, respectful communication is vital for effective discipline.

Stay calm and composed: Managing your emotions is as important as managing your child's behavior. Displaying calmness and composure, even in challenging behavior, models emotional regulation for your child.

Teach empathy and respect: Encourage your child to consider the feelings and perspectives of others, and this will foster empathy, respect, and kindness.

Promote self-discipline: Ultimately, the goal is to help your child develop self-discipline. Please encourage them to think about their actions, consider the potential consequences, and make choices based on their understanding of right and wrong.

Remember that every child is unique, and what works for one may not work for another. Tailoring your approach to your child's needs and personality is essential. The key is to be patient, consistent, and loving, always keeping in mind that the ultimate goal of discipline is to guide your child toward becoming a responsible, empathetic, and self-reliant individual.

Moreover, remember that as a single parent, you're the primary role model for your child. Your actions, reactions, and how you treat others will profoundly influence your child's behavior. So, always strive to exemplify the values and behaviors you want your child to emulate.

Encouraging Emotional Resilience and Independence

As a single parent, one of your paramount goals is to nurture your child's emotional resilience and foster their independence. These traits prepare your child for life's inevitable ups and downs and build self-confidence, self-reliance, and a sense of personal responsibility.

Emotional resilience refers to one's ability to adapt to stressful situations or crises, and it's the capacity to bounce back from difficult experiences and maintain balance in adversity. Fostering emotional resilience in your child equips them with tools to navigate the challenges they encounter throughout life, from minor disappointments to significant setbacks.

Normalize Emotions: The first step towards nurturing emotional resilience is to create an environment where all feelings are validated and accepted. Please encourage your child to express their feelings freely and reassure them that feeling angry, sad, or scared is okay. Normalizing emotions helps children to understand that it's not the feelings that are problematic but how we manage them.

Teach Emotional Regulation: Teach your child strategies to manage their emotions effectively. These could include deep-breathing exercises, physical activities, creative outlets like drawing or writing, or simply cooling down. Show them that while we can't always control what we feel, we can control how we react to our feelings.

Problem-Solving Skills: Encourage your child to develop solutions for problems or conflicts. Instead of rushing to solve their problems, guide them through brainstorming solutions, weighing the pros and cons, and making decisions. This will enhance their problem-solving skills and foster a sense of independence.

On the other hand, independence involves cultivating a sense of self-reliance and personal responsibility in your child. It's about teaching them the necessary skills to care for themselves and make sound decisions independently. Here's how you can encourage independence in your child:

Gradual Release of Responsibility: Start by assigning your child age-appropriate tasks and responsibilities, like tidying their room, making their bed, or helping with household chores. Gradually increase these responsibilities as they grow older and more capable.

Encourage Decision-Making: Allow your child to make choices appropriate to their age and maturity level. This could be as simple as choosing their outfit for the day or deciding which homework assignment to tackle first. Decision-making fosters a sense of control and teaches them to accept the consequences of their choices.

Teach Life Skills: Equip your child with essential life skills, such as cooking, cleaning, managing money, and basic problem-solving. These skills will boost their confidence and prepare them for adulthood.

Resist the Urge to Overprotect: While it's natural to want to shield your child from harm or disappointment, it's crucial to resist the urge to overprotect. Let them experience the natural consequences of their actions, as this is often the best way to learn.

By fostering emotional resilience and independence in your child, you're equipping them with essential tools for success in all areas of life.

7. Navigating the Educational System

The quote "Remember that one is not half of two; two are halves of one." by the poet E.E. Cummings might seem outside of education at first glance. However, it beautifully captures the essence of our seventh chapter: Navigating the Educational System. As a single parent, you are not just half of what a two-parent family can offer - you are whole in and of yourself.

You possess the capacity to guide your child's educational journey with determination and resilience. This chapter will equip you with practical knowledge and strategies to help you choose the right school for your child, support their academic success, collaborate effectively with teachers, comprehend the nuances of special education and Individualized Education Programs (IEPs), and actively engage in your child's extracurricular activities. Education is a shared journey, and you can lead the way.

Choosing the Right School for Your Child

Selecting the right school for your child is a pivotal decision. As a single parent, the weight of this decision may feel even more significant. A school's environment, curriculum, and values can significantly influence your child's development and future academic success.

Understand Your Child's Needs

Firstly, it's crucial to understand your child's individual needs, talents, and interests. Every child is unique, and the best school for one may not be the best for another. Some children might thrive in a structured, traditional academic setting, while others may flourish in a more creative, project-based environment.

Consider the following points:

- Does your child have special educational needs that should be catered to?

- Does your child excel in a particular area, such as the arts, sciences, or sports?

- What is your child's learning style? Are they visual, auditory, or kinesthetic learners?

Research Schools in Your Area

Once you have a clear understanding of your child's needs, it's time to research the schools available in your area. Public, private, charter, and magnet schools offer unique advantages and disadvantages.

Consider the following:

- What curriculum does the school follow?

- What is the school's reputation and rating?

- What is the student-teacher ratio?

- What extracurricular activities are offered?

- How does the school support children with special educational needs?

Visit and Engage

Finally, try to visit the schools that you are considering. Meet the teachers, talk to the students, and observe the general atmosphere of the school. Ask about the school's policy on parental involvement, their approach to discipline, and their strategies for fostering student growth.

Remember, it's not just about finding the "best" school—it's about finding the right school for your unique child. Being a single parent doesn't mean you must navigate this process alone. Contact your support networks, other parents, and educational professionals for advice and support.

Supporting Your Child's Academic Success

As a single parent, balancing your responsibilities can be challenging. Nonetheless, your role in your child's academic success is pivotal.

Establishing a Supportive Home Environment

A conducive home environment is the bedrock of academic success, which involves creating a space that encourages learning, curiosity, and creativity.

- Dedicate a quiet, well-lit space for study and homework.

- Ensure that educational resources, such as books, games, and online learning tools, are accessible.

- Set consistent homework, reading, and bedtime routines to help your child manage their time effectively.

Encouraging a Love for Learning

- Fostering a genuine love for learning can help motivate your child to excel academically.

- Show interest in what they're learning by asking about their school day.

- Encourage curiosity and critical thinking by asking open-ended questions.

- Praise effort, not just achievement, to promote a growth mindset.

Engaging with Schoolwork

Being involved in your child's schoolwork doesn't mean doing the work for them but guiding and supporting them.

- Review homework assignments with your child, offering assistance when needed.

- Encourage them to ask for help when they don't understand something.

- Reinforce what they learn at school with related activities at home.

Communicating with Teachers

Regular communication with your child's teachers can provide valuable insights into their academic progress.

- Attend parent-teacher meetings and stay updated on your child's progress.

- Don't hesitate to reach out to teachers with any concerns or questions.

- Collaborate with teachers to support your child's learning at home.

Supporting your child's academic success is a journey, not a destination, and it's about creating an environment that nurtures growth, celebrates progress, and fosters resilience. As a single parent, your unwavering support can make all the difference in your child's academic journey.

Parent-Teacher Collaboration and Involvement

Building a strong parent-teacher partnership supports your child's academic journey and allows for better understanding, communication, and collaboration in service of your child's education.

Importance of Parent-Teacher Collaboration

The importance of parent-teacher collaboration cannot be overstated. Teachers provide a valuable perspective on your child's academic progress, behavior, and social interactions, and they can offer insights that you, as a parent, may not observe at home.

Establishing Communication Channels

Establishing open and regular communication channels is the first step in forging a good relationship with your child's teachers. This could be through emails, phone calls, scheduled meetings, or parent-teacher conferences.

- Ensure the teacher has your contact information.

- Reach out to the teacher at the beginning of the school year to introduce yourself.

- Keep lines of communication open and approachable.

Active Involvement in School Activities

Being actively involved in your child's school activities can foster a strong parent-teacher relationship. This could include attending school events, volunteering for classroom activities, or participating in parent-teacher associations.

- Attend school events and parent-teacher meetings regularly.

- Volunteer for activities in your child's class when possible.

- Join the parent-teacher association to stay informed and involved.

Collaborating on Educational Goals

Lastly, collaborate with your child's teachers to set and achieve educational goals. These goals can cover academic progress, behavior, social skills, or any other areas of concern.

- Discuss your child's strengths and areas of improvement with the teacher.

- Collaborate on setting realistic and achievable goals for your child.

- Regularly review and adjust these goals based on your child's progress.

Remember, a strong parent-teacher partnership is a two-way street. It requires open communication, mutual respect, and a shared commitment to your child's educational success. As a single parent, your active involvement can significantly enhance this relationship, providing your child with a supportive academic network.

Understanding Special Education and IEPs

Special Education and Individualized Education Programs (IEPs) ensure that all children receive the support they need to thrive academically. Understanding these resources can empower you to advocate for your child effectively as a single parent.

Introduction to Special Education

Special education refers to tailored instruction and services provided to students with disabilities, learning differences, or other special needs.

- It covers various services, from modified instruction in the regular classroom to specialized programs.

- The goal is to ensure that all children have equal learning opportunities and success.

The Role of IEPs

An Individualized Education Program (IEP) is a legal document outlining the specific Special Education services a child will receive.

- It includes the child's present academic and functional performance levels, annual goals, services provided, and how progress will be measured.

- It is developed by a team that includes parents, teachers, school administrators, and other relevant professionals.

Navigating the IEP Process

Getting an IEP for your child can be daunting, but remember, you are an integral part of this process.

- If you suspect your child might benefit from Special Education services, the first step is to request an evaluation.

- If the evaluation confirms your child requires additional support, you'll be involved in creating the IEP.

- The IEP is reviewed at least once a year, but you can request a review at any time if you believe changes are needed.

Advocating for Your Child

As a single parent, advocating for your child in the Special Education process can feel overwhelming.

- Familiarize yourself with your child's rights under the Individuals with Disabilities Education Act (IDEA).

- Consider seeking support from a Special Education advocate or attorney if needed.

- Always remember, you know your child best and are their strongest advocate.

Understanding Special Education and IEPs allows you to advocate for your child. The goal is not to label or limit your child but to provide them with the necessary resources to succeed. Your informed voice and advocacy can significantly impact your child's educational journey.

Engaging in Your Child's Extracurricular Activities

Extracurricular activities are an integral part of a well-rounded education, and they can foster social skills, creativity, teamwork, and self-esteem. As a single parent, your support and involvement in these activities can significantly enhance your child's experience.

The Importance of Extracurricular Activities

Extracurricular activities offer opportunities for your child to explore interests outside of the academic curriculum, develop new skills, and build relationships.

- They may include sports, clubs, art, music, drama, community service, and more.
- They can be crucial to your child's personal and social development.

Choosing the Right Activities

Selecting suitable activities depends on your child's interests, abilities, and schedule.

- Encourage your child to try different activities to discover their passions.
- Be mindful of the time commitment to balance schoolwork and extracurricular activities.

Your Role as a Parent

As a parent, your role is to support and encourage your child in their chosen activities.

- Be there for your child, whether attending games, performances, or club meetings.

- Show interest in their activity by asking about their experiences and progress.

- Celebrate their efforts and achievements, regardless of the outcome.

Balancing Commitments

It's important to help your child balance their academic responsibilities with their extracurricular commitments.

- Help them manage their time effectively.

- Encourage them to prioritize their tasks and commitments.

- Ensure they have enough downtime to relax and unwind.

Involvement in your child's extracurricular activities does not only mean being physically present at their events but also being emotionally supportive of their efforts and achievements. Engaging in your child's extracurricular activities shows them that you value their interests and support their holistic development. This involvement can create a lasting positive impact on your child's self-esteem and motivation.

8. Maintaining Mental and Emotional Well-being

As a single parent, you carry an immense responsibility. You juggle work, household chores, and parenting, often without the immediate support of a partner. This can, at times, be an overwhelming experience. This chapter addresses the importance of maintaining mental and emotional well-being amidst the complexities of single parenthood. The focus on self-care is not a luxury but a necessary aspect of your life that allows you to function optimally and provide the best care for your children.

Self-Care for Single Parents

Taking care of yourself is not just about maintaining your physical health; it's about nurturing your emotional, mental, and spiritual well-being. As a single parent, it's easy to let self-care fall by the wayside as you focus on caring for your children's needs. However, it would be best if you prioritized your well-being to be your best parent.

Self-care starts with the basics: getting enough sleep, maintaining a balanced diet, and incorporating regular physical activity into your routine. Lack of sleep, poor nutrition, and physical inactivity can all contribute to feelings of fatigue and stress, making it harder to manage the demands of single parenthood.

Beyond the basics, self-care also involves activities that you enjoy and that help you relax and recharge. This could be anything from reading a book, taking a leisurely walk, meditating, or spending time with friends. Find what works for you and make it a non-negotiable part of your routine.

One of the challenges single parents often face is a need for more time for self-care. However, remember that self-care doesn't have to be time-consuming. Even a few minutes of deep breathing or a quick walk around the block can help reduce stress and improve your mood.

Another crucial aspect of self-care is setting boundaries. This can mean learning to say no to additional responsibilities that could lead to overwhelming or setting aside quiet time for yourself each day, free from interruptions.

Maintaining your mental and emotional health isn't selfish; it's essential. You're improving your children's well-being and modeling healthy habits by caring for yourself.

Managing Stress and Overwhelm

The role of a single parent is multifaceted and can, at times, be stress-inducing. You may be dealing with work demands, financial stress, household maintenance, and meeting your children's needs, all while trying to find time for yourself. When stress and overwhelm become chronic, it can impact your mental and physical health (American Psychological Association, 2020). Therefore, learning to manage stress effectively is a critical aspect of maintaining your overall well-being.

Start by recognizing the signs of stress, which may include irritability, difficulty sleeping, feeling overwhelmed, or changes in appetite. Becoming aware of these signs can help you take steps to manage stress before it escalates.

There are several strategies to help manage stress effectively:

Mindfulness and relaxation techniques: These include practices such as deep breathing, progressive muscle relaxation, and mindfulness meditation. These techniques can help reduce feelings of stress and promote a sense of calm (Goyal et al., 2014).

Physical activity: Regular exercise can help reduce stress and improve mood by triggering the release of endorphins, often termed the body's "feel-good" hormones (Childs & de Wit, 2014).

Social support: Connecting with friends, family, or support groups can provide emotional assistance and a sense of belonging. Sometimes, simply sharing your experiences and feelings with others can provide relief.

Time management: Effective time management can reduce feelings of overwhelm. Prioritize tasks, delegate when possible, and remember that leaving some tasks undone is okay.

Remember, it's normal to feel overwhelmed at times, but if feelings of stress persist, it may be beneficial to seek professional support.

Seeking Professional Support and Therapy

As a single parent, you may face unique challenges affecting your mental and emotional well-being. While the support of friends and family is invaluable, there may be times when you need to seek professional help to manage your emotions and mental health effectively.

Professional support can take various forms, including individual therapy, support groups, or counseling sessions. Here are some reasons why you might consider seeking professional help:

Persistent feelings of stress, anxiety, or depression: If you're struggling with these emotions, and they're affecting your daily life, it's essential to seek help from a mental health professional. They can help you identify the sources of your stress and provide strategies to cope with them effectively.

Grief and loss: Losing a partner or other significant life changes can be emotionally challenging. A therapist or counselor can help you process these emotions and support you as you navigate the grieving process.

Parenting challenges: Parenting can be difficult, and seeking professional guidance can help you develop effective strategies for managing behavioral issues, setting boundaries, and fostering a healthy parent-child relationship.

Balancing work and family life: A professional can help you balance your work and family responsibilities, preventing burnout and promoting overall well-being.

Coping with isolation: Single parents may sometimes feel isolated or disconnected from their peers. Support groups or therapy can allow you to share your experiences and connect with others in similar situations.

Remember, seeking help is a sign of strength, not weakness. By addressing your emotional needs and seeking professional support, you're taking an essential step in ensuring your overall well-being and becoming a more resilient and effective parent.

Balancing Personal Life and Parenthood

One of the unique challenges of single parenthood is balancing parenting responsibilities with personal needs and interests. It's essential to remember that you are not just a parent but also an individual with personal goals, hobbies, and friendships outside your parent role.

Balancing personal life and parenthood isn't always easy, but here are some strategies that can help:

Prioritize self-care: As mentioned earlier, self-care is not a luxury but a necessity. Prioritize time for activities that you enjoy and that contribute to your well-being.

Create a routine: A well-structured routine can bring order to chaos, reducing stress and creating predictability for you and your children. While creating the routine, carve out time for yourself.

Seek support: Don't hesitate to accept help from friends, family, or childcare services. This can provide you with some much-needed time for rest, relaxation, or personal pursuits.

Stay socially connected: Maintain your relationships with friends and enjoy social activities. Social connections can provide emotional support and help reduce feelings of isolation.

Set personal goals: Whether it's a fitness goal, a professional goal, or learning a new skill, setting personal goals can help maintain your individuality and provide a sense of achievement outside of your parenting role.

Remember, maintaining a balance between personal life and parenthood is not about perfection but creating a sustainable and enjoyable life for you and your children. You deserve time for yourself, and taking that time makes you a happier, more well-rounded parent.

Recognizing and Addressing Signs of Parental Burnout

Parental burnout is a state of physical, emotional, and mental exhaustion resulting from prolonged stress and high demands associated with parenting. It's not uncommon for single parents to experience burnout due to their unique pressures and responsibilities.

Recognizing the signs of parental burnout is the first step toward addressing it. These signs can include:

- Feeling constantly tired, even after a good night's sleep.

- Feeling detached or distant from your children, or less joy in parenting than you used to.

- Feeling overwhelmed by your parenting responsibilities and feeling like you can't keep up.

- Increased irritability and impatience with your children.

- Changes in sleep or appetite, either sleeping and eating too much or too little.

- If you recognize these signs, it's essential to take steps to address burnout:

Practice self-care: Prioritize activities that help you relax and rejuvenate, such as exercise, a healthy diet, adequate sleep, and hobbies or interests you enjoy.

Seek support: Reach out to friends, family, support groups, or a mental health professional. Sharing your feelings and experiences can provide relief and practical solutions.

Set boundaries: Learn to avoid additional responsibilities that could add to the stress. Make sure you have some time each day that's just for you.

Practice mindfulness: Techniques such as deep breathing, meditation, or yoga can help reduce stress and promote a sense of calm.

Get professional help: If feelings of burnout persist, consider seeking help from a professional. Therapists or counselors can provide strategies to manage stress and avoid burnout.

Remember, experiencing parental burnout doesn't make you a bad parent. It's a sign that you're human and carrying a heavy load. By recognizing and addressing the signs of burnout, you're taking a crucial step toward maintaining your well-being and continuing to be your best parent.

9. Building a Strong Parent-Child Bond

The parent-child bond is a unique relationship filled with unconditional love, mutual respect, and shared joy. It lays the foundation for a child's emotional well-being, social relationships, and overall development. For single parents, building a strong parent-child bond is crucial for providing emotional security and fostering their children's resilience, self-esteem, and life skills.

The Importance of Quality Time

Quality time is the heart of a strong parent-child relationship. During these moments, bonds are formed, trust is established, and memories are created. For single parents, juggling numerous responsibilities might limit their time with their children. However, it's essential to realize that it's not the quantity but the quality of time that truly matters.

Making the Most of Your Time Together

While spending large blocks of time together may be challenging, you can find moments to connect with your child throughout the day. These could be shared meals, bedtime stories, or a walk to the park. What's important is that you are fully present, engaged, and attentive to your child during these times.

Creating Meaningful Experiences

Quality time also involves creating meaningful experiences with your child. It's not about extravagant outings or expensive gifts but the simple joys of being together. You might cook a meal together, play a board game, or read a favorite book. These shared experiences will help your child feel loved, appreciated, and connected to you.

Consistency is Key

Consistency is another crucial element of quality time. A regular schedule for shared activities can give your child a sense of security and predictability. It could be a weekly movie night, a daily bedtime story, or a monthly 'day out.'

This routine can also remind you to take a break from your busy schedule and focus solely on your child.

Effective Communication with Your Child

Communication forms the backbone of a strong parent-child relationship, promoting mutual understanding, building trust, and fostering emotional intimacy. As a single parent, effective communication with your child is even more crucial as it allows you to understand their feelings, worries, and needs.

Fostering Open Communication

Open communication begins with creating an environment where your child feels safe expressing their thoughts and emotions. Encourage them to share their daily experiences, dreams, fears, and feelings. Assure them that their thoughts matter and that you are always there to listen.

Active Listening

Listening is an integral part of communication. Active listening involves hearing your child's words and understanding their emotions and viewpoints. It means acknowledging their feelings, asking open-ended questions, and showing empathy. This level of engagement shows your child that their thoughts and feelings are important to you.

Nonverbal Communication

Nonverbal cues can sometimes tell more than words. Pay attention to your child's body language, facial expressions, and tone of voice. These can provide insight into their emotions and mental state. Similarly, be aware of your nonverbal signals, as they can significantly influence your communication with your child.

Constructive Feedback

There will be times when you need to provide feedback or correction. Ensure this is done constructively, focusing on the behavior, not the child. Provide clear, specific feedback and guide them towards better choices in the future.

Supporting Your Child Through Life Transitions

Life transitions, both big and small, can be challenging for children. These changes can range from starting a new school or moving to a new city to more personal shifts like the onset of adolescence or dealing with the loss of a loved one. As a single parent, your support during these transitions is invaluable.

Understanding the Impact of Change

Firstly, it's essential to understand the impact of these changes on your child. While some children may adjust quickly, others may struggle. Look out for signs of stress or anxiety and be prepared to offer additional support during these periods.

Open Conversations about Change

Discussing upcoming changes can help alleviate some of your child's fear and anxiety. Provide age-appropriate information and answer any questions they may have. Reassure them that feeling uncertain or scared is okay and that you're there to support them.

Providing Stability and Routine

Despite the changes, maintain as much stability and routine as possible. Familiar routines can provide a sense of security amidst the uncertainties of change. Simple things like maintaining mealtimes, bedtimes, or weekly activities may offer a sense of continuity.

Emotional Support

Emotional support is crucial during transitions. Let your child express their feelings without judgment. Validate their emotions and reassure them that their feelings are normal. Encourage them to use healthy coping strategies to deal with their emotions.

Celebrating Achievements and Milestones Together

Recognizing and celebrating your child's achievements and milestones is integral to building a strong parent-child bond. It shows your child that you are invested in their growth and development and bolsters their self-esteem and confidence.

The Power of Acknowledgment

Acknowledgment of success, no matter how small, reinforces positive behavior and instills a sense of accomplishment in your child. Praise their effort, not just the outcome. Emphasize the dedication, hard work, or creativity they've put into achieving their goal.

Marking Milestones

Life is filled with milestones, each a step towards growth and independence. Whether it's the first day at school, graduation, or a first job, these events deserve recognition. Celebrate these moments and express your pride in your child's achievements.

Creating Celebration Rituals

Creating celebration rituals can be a fun and meaningful way to honor achievements and milestones. It could be a special dinner at their favorite restaurant, a family outing, or even a small gift symbolizing accomplishment. These rituals not only celebrate the achievement but also create lasting memories.

Balancing Praise and Constructive Feedback

While it's important to celebrate achievements, it's equally essential to provide constructive feedback. This helps your child understand that mistakes and failures are part of learning, promoting resilience and a growth mindset.

Cultivating Shared Interests and Hobbies

Developing shared interests and hobbies is a rewarding way to bond with your child, and it provides a platform for quality time, mutual enjoyment, and learning from each other.

Identifying Shared Interests

Begin by identifying activities that both you and your child enjoy. It could be anything from gardening, painting, playing a musical instrument, or cooking. The aim is not to impose your interests on your child but to find common ground you can explore and enjoy together.

Fostering a Learning Environment

Encourage a learning environment where you can grow and learn from each other. If your child is interested in digital art and you have traditional painting skills, you could learn about digital art from your child while teaching them about color theory and brush techniques.

Making Time for Shared Activities

Life as a single parent can be hectic, but it's essential to carve out time for these shared activities. This could be a few hours during the weekend or a designated time in the evening. Consistency is key in making this a special time for both of you.

Benefits of Shared Interests

Shared interests and hobbies offer various benefits. They can help in relieving stress, promoting open communication, and creating a sense of camaraderie. They also provide opportunities to create shared memories, strengthening your bond over time.

10. Social Life and Dating as a Single Parent

Embarking on the journey of single parenthood can often be accompanied by significant changes in your social life. The connections you once had might shift, your free time could be reduced, and your focus may predominantly be on your children. However, your social life and the possibility of dating as a single parent are still very much within reach. This chapter serves as a beacon of light, gently illuminating your path toward balancing parenting duties while reclaiming your social life, embracing new friendships, and even exploring the realm of dating. Remember, taking care of your social and emotional needs is not an act of selfishness but rather an essential part of maintaining your overall well-being.

Rebuilding Your Social Circle

As a single parent, it's crucial to remember that maintaining a healthy social circle isn't a luxury but a necessity. Balancing the roles of a caregiver, provider, and often the primary disciplinarian can sometimes be isolating. Still, you can find emotional and practical support by rebuilding your social circle.

Starting afresh with your social life often involves making new connections and rekindling old ones. It may initially seem daunting, but remember, many had walked this path before and emerged stronger and happier. Let's explore how you can begin this process.

Find Your Community

Parent Groups: Connect with other single parents who can relate to your experiences. Numerous online and offline groups provide an excellent platform for this. Share your triumphs, trials, and tips, and create a support network.

Neighborhood Associations or Clubs: Consider joining local organizations, community projects, or hobby clubs in your area. These groups can provide a sense of belonging and can also be a source of practical support.

Children's School or Activity Groups: By engaging with your child's school PTA, sports clubs, or other activity groups, you can build relationships with other parents. Remember, these groups are not just for your children but can also serve as a valuable social lifeline for you.

Reignite Old Friendships

It's easy to lose touch with old friends when life changes drastically. However, reaching out to these individuals can help reestablish those meaningful connections. An understanding friend can offer a listening ear, a shoulder to lean on, or even a well-timed laugh when needed.

Make Time for Social Activities

The demands of single parenting can often leave little time for socializing. However, setting aside time for social activities is vital for your well-being. It's important to schedule regular 'me time' that allows you to relax, have fun, and engage with others.

Cultivate Your Interests

Join clubs or groups related to your hobbies or passions. This offers you an opportunity to do something you love and allows you to meet like-minded people. Whether it's a book club, a hiking group, or a cooking class, following your interests can lead to rewarding social connections.

Nurture the Relationships You Have

Friendships require nurturing to thrive. Make it a point to keep in touch, show up when needed, and offer support to your friends. A mutual exchange is the cornerstone of any lasting relationship.

A single mother of two, Sandra felt isolated and overwhelmed after her divorce. She mustered the courage to join a local single parents' group. Not only did this group provide her with a sense of community and support, but it also gave her access to practical advice and resources. Furthermore, engaging with her son's soccer team parents gave her a fresh perspective and new friendships. Sandra's story illustrates that actively seeking out and nurturing relationships can rebuild your social circle as a single parent.

The journey to rebuilding your social life can be rewarding. It may take time and patience, but remember; the aim is to create a supportive network around you that enriches your life and provides the emotional and practical support that all parents need.

Navigating the Dating World

Finding your footing in the dating world can be exciting and challenging as a single parent. While new relationships offer the joy of companionship, they also raise questions about introducing new partners to your children, balancing your time between parenting and dating, and maintaining your individuality. This section aims to guide you through these intricacies and offer practical advice for navigating the dating world.

Be Ready

Before embarking on your dating journey, it's essential to ensure that you're emotionally ready. Healing from past relationships and creating stability for yourself and your children is paramount. There's no timeline to follow; it's about when you feel comfortable and ready to welcome someone new into your life.

Take It Slow

There's no need to rush when introducing a new partner to your children. It's essential to ensure the relationship is stable and has long-term potential before bringing someone new into your children's lives. Taking it slow allows everyone to adjust to the new circumstances gradually.

Balance Your Time

Balancing your time between dating and parenting can be a challenge, but it's important to remember that you're not alone in this. You can:

- Consider scheduling dates when your children are engaged in their activities or staying with the other parent if that's an option.

- Utilize online dating, which allows you to connect with people at your own pace and in your own time.

Communicate Clearly

Honesty and transparency are essential in any relationship, particularly when dating as a single parent. Ensure your potential partner understands your role as a parent and what it entails. Communicating your and your children's needs and setting clear boundaries is crucial.

Keep Your Interests Alive

Maintaining your hobbies and interests is important even when you're dating. This helps you keep your individuality and ensures your life is balanced and fulfilling.

To illustrate these points, let's consider the story of David, a single father of one who decided to reenter the dating world. David ensured he was emotionally ready before he started dating, ensuring he could offer his daughter and potential partner a stable environment. He took it slow, and when he did meet someone he was serious about, he communicated his needs and responsibilities as a single father. He also maintained his interests, keeping up with his love for painting and hiking, ensuring a balanced life.

David's story is a testament that, with patience and careful navigation, dating as a single parent is possible and can bring joy and companionship into your life.

Navigating the dating world as a single parent requires a balance of patience, communication, and care for yourself and your children. It may present its challenges but also holds the potential for newfound joy and companionship. Remember, your journey is unique, and there's no rush or right way to navigate it. Your focus should always be on what's best for you and your family's emotional health and well-being.

The journey of single parenting is no less than an adventure - full of surprises, hurdles, and triumphs. While taking care of your child's physical needs may seem like a task, understanding and supporting their emotional needs is equally significant in their well-being. This chapter is dedicated to aiding you in understanding your child's emotions, helping them cope with separation or divorce, and fostering healthy relationships with both parents. Remember, your child's emotional health is a cornerstone for their overall development, shaping their personality and future relationships.

11. Supporting Your Child's Emotional Needs

As single parents, we understand that the responsibility might feel immense, and the combined roles of a nurturer, provider, and protector may sometimes feel overwhelming. But rest assured, your love, patience, and perseverance are the most powerful tools to help you navigate this journey successfully. This chapter will equip you with practical strategies and actionable advice to nurture your child's emotional health. It will help you create a safe and supportive environment where your child can express their feelings, discuss their fears, and grow confidently. Regardless of your circumstances or background, remember you're not alone in this journey; each step taken is a stride towards a happier and healthier relationship with your child.

Understanding Your Child's Emotions

Understanding your child's emotions can often seem like learning a new language. This task can feel particularly challenging as a single parent, but gaining this insight is essential to supporting your child's emotional well-being. It's important to remember that emotions are a natural response to life experiences, and how your child communicates these feelings will evolve.

The first step is to create an open and trusting environment where your child feels comfortable expressing their feelings. Let them know that all emotions, whether happiness, sadness, anger, or fear, are valid and natural responses to different situations. This validation encourages open dialogue and helps your child feel understood and accepted.

Here are some practical strategies to help you understand your child's emotions:

Active Listening: This means giving your full attention to your child when they're expressing their feelings. Put away distractions, maintain eye contact, and use nonverbal cues like nodding to show that you're fully engaged.

Empathy: Try to put yourself in your child's shoes and understand their perspective. Expressing empathy can look like saying, "I can see that you're upset because your friend didn't share the toy with you."

Emotion Coaching: Help your child identify and label their emotions. For instance, you might say, "You look frustrated, and is it because you're finding this puzzle difficult?" This gives children a language to articulate their feelings and makes it easier to communicate their emotions in the future.

Observe Non-Verbal Cues: Pay attention to your child's body language, facial expressions, and behavior, which can provide valuable clues about their emotional state.

Encourage Expression Through Creative Outlets: Not all children can express their feelings verbally. Encourage them to express their emotions using creative outlets like drawing, writing, or role-playing.

Remember that every child is unique, and how they express their emotions can vary widely. It's okay if you don't always understand your child's emotions perfectly, and the most important thing is to show that you care for them and try to understand. As you progress in your journey of single parenting, these skills of understanding your child's emotions will strengthen your bond and enable you to provide the emotional support your child needs.

Helping Your Child Cope with Separation or Divorce

Separation or divorce can be a tumultuous time for a child, stirring up emotions from confusion and anger to sadness and fear. As a single parent, you guide your child through this challenging period. It may not always be easy, but you can help them navigate these uncharted emotional waters with love, patience, and understanding.

The key to helping your child cope is maintaining stability while acknowledging their feelings about the separation or divorce. This validation reassures your child that their emotions are valid and they're not alone in this process.

Here are some actionable tips to help your child cope with the reality of

separation or divorce:

Maintain Routines: Keep daily routines and schedules as consistent as possible. This stability can provide comfort to your child during a time when many other things are changing.

Honesty and Open Communication: Have age-appropriate discussions about the changes in your family structure. Use simple, clear language to explain what is happening and reassure them that both parents still love and will always be there for them.

Avoid Blaming or Negative Talk: Never use your child to vent about the other parent. It's essential to separate your feelings from your role as a parent.

Reassurance: Repeatedly reassure your child that they are not the cause of the separation or divorce. Children often blame themselves for these situations, so it's crucial to emphasize that this isn't the case.

Encourage Expression of Feelings: Allow your child to express their feelings about the separation or divorce without judgment. Validate their feelings and remind them it's okay to feel upset, confused, or angry.

Seek Professional Help if Needed: If your child struggles to cope, consider seeking help from a professional counselor or therapist. They can provide valuable tools and strategies to help your child process their feelings.

Navigating the path of separation or divorce is a journey, not a destination. It's perfectly normal for ups and downs along the way. Most importantly, your child feels loved, supported, and heard. As a single parent, your unwavering presence and understanding during this period can significantly influence your child's ability to adjust and thrive amidst these changes.

Fostering Healthy Relationships with Both Parents

Regardless of the circumstances that led to single parenthood, fostering a healthy relationship between your child and both parents is crucial for their emotional well-being. Children benefit from maintaining strong, positive relationships with both parents, and it's essential to facilitate this to the best of your ability. This task might be challenging, especially when dealing with personal emotions and difficult situations, but it's undeniably worth the effort.

Here's some practical and actionable advice to help you nurture these vital relationships:

Encourage Regular Communication: Facilitate regular contact between your child and the other parent. This could include phone calls, video chats, emails, or letters. The goal is to keep the lines of communication open, which benefits your child's emotional well-being.

Promote Positive Talk: Always speak positively about the other parent in front of your child. Regardless of your personal feelings, separating them from your child's relationship with their other parent is important. Negative talk can impact your child's perception and potentially damage their relationship with the other parent.

Support Their Bond: Encourage activities that strengthen the bond between your child and the other parent. This could be a shared hobby, a regular outing, or even a special routine they have together.

Resolve Disputes Respectfully: Disagreements are inevitable, but they should be handled away from your child. Never use your child as a messenger or involve them in adult issues, and it's important to shield them from conflict as much as possible.

Flexibility: Be flexible with visitation schedules when feasible. Understand that circumstances can change, and the other parent needs quality time with her child.

Co-Parenting or Parallel Parenting: Consider a co-parenting or parallel parenting strategy depending on your relationship with the other parent. Co-parenting involves active communication and collaboration on parenting decisions, while parallel parenting involves disengagement from each other and limited direct contact, with both parents independently guiding their child's life.

Fostering a healthy relationship with both parents requires patience, understanding, and flexibility. You may sometimes face obstacles, but remember, the ultimate goal is to create a stable, loving environment for your child. While this chapter in your life may present challenges, your commitment to your child's emotional health and happiness will guide you through. Remember, you're not alone in this journey; each step you take is a stride toward fostering healthy, long-lasting relationships for your child.

12. Dealing with Extended Family and In-Laws

As we journey deeper into the labyrinth of single parenting, we must now consider the broader ecosystem influencing your child's life – your extended family and in-laws. It is irrefutable that extended family members and in-laws can play a significant role in shaping your child's development. They represent different facets of family life, diverse viewpoints, and unique experiences your child can learn and grow from. But as a single parent, managing these relationships can feel like a tightrope. This chapter aims to equip you with the necessary skills to navigate these relationships, creating a healthier environment for you and your child.

At the heart of these familial interactions are two key components: setting boundaries and handling conflict and criticism. Though beautiful, family ties can become complicated when boundaries are breached or there's a conflict or undue criticism.

As a single parent, you bear a dual burden – you must simultaneously maintain your sanity and your child's emotional health. By learning to set appropriate boundaries with extended family members, you can ensure that their involvement is a source of support, not stress. Additionally, effectively managing criticism and conflict can create a nurturing and accepting environment for your child to thrive. So, let's delve into the nuances of these aspects in the ensuing sections.

Setting Boundaries with Extended Family Members

As a single parent, setting boundaries with extended family members is essential to establishing a supportive environment for your child. Boundaries can foster understanding, protect your space, and define acceptable behavior within family dynamics. However, setting these boundaries can be challenging and require a nuanced approach.

Let's walk through the steps to effectively set these boundaries:

Step 1: Self-Assessment

Start by understanding your own needs and limitations. Are there specific areas or subjects you'd like to remain untouched by family members? Is there a level of involvement that feels too intrusive? These questions help define what is acceptable for you and your child and where you need to draw lines.

Step 2: Clear Communication

Once you understand your boundaries, it's time to express them to your family. This may be uncomfortable initially, but effective communication is the bedrock of healthy relationships. Be honest and firm, yet respectful, in your approach. Let them know what you are comfortable with, what feels intrusive, and why these boundaries are necessary for your well-being and your child's.

Step 3: Reinforcement

Once you've communicated your boundaries, the challenge is to maintain them. This can be particularly tough when dealing with pushback. Stay firm and consistent with your expectations. Remember, you're protecting your peace and creating a healthier environment for your child.

Step 4: Evaluate and Adjust

Lastly, review the effectiveness of your boundaries regularly. Are they serving their purpose? Are they being respected? If you find certain boundaries need to be fixed or new ones need to be established, feel free to reassess and make necessary adjustments.

However, setting boundaries is not just a series of steps but an ongoing process. Here are some additional tips that can help you navigate this journey:

Respect their feelings: Your extended family members or in-laws may have strong feelings about their involvement in your child's life. It's important to acknowledge these feelings while maintaining your boundaries.

Seek professional help if necessary: If setting boundaries leads to significant conflict or stress, seeking help from a professional, such as a family counselor or therapist, might be beneficial.

Model boundaries for your child: By setting and maintaining your boundaries, you're also teaching your child an important lesson about respecting personal space and autonomy. This will be an invaluable skill for them in their relationships.

As circumstances change and your child grows, you should revisit and renegotiate these boundaries. This fluidity is a natural part of the process. Let's explore a few scenarios that you might encounter and discuss how to handle them:

Scenario 1: Overstepping of Boundaries

Despite your best efforts, there will likely be instances when a family member oversteps a boundary. When this happens, address the issue promptly and clearly. Use "I" statements to express your feelings and reiterate the importance of the boundary that has been crossed.

For example, if an in-law insists on disciplining your child against your wishes, you could say, "I understand you have your perspective, but I feel uncomfortable when you discipline my child. As a parent, I believe it's my responsibility to guide them."

Scenario 2: Boundary Testing

Family members might sometimes test the boundaries to see if they hold firm. In these situations, consistency is critical. Reinforce the boundary gently yet firmly, emphasizing that it's in place for your and your child's well-being.

For instance, if a relative continuously offers unsolicited advice, you might respond, "I appreciate your concern and advice, but I prefer to discuss other topics. Let's enjoy our time together."

Scenario 3: Feelings of Exclusion

Boundaries can sometimes be misconstrued as exclusion, particularly if they were set after a significant change in the family dynamics, like a divorce or a death. In these situations, it's crucial to reaffirm the value of the family member's relationship with your child while asserting the boundary.

For example, if a family member feels excluded from decision-making, you could say, "I value your input and care for my child, but as their parent, the final decisions must lie with me. This doesn't reduce your importance in their life."

Scenario 4: Guilt and Pressure

Dealing with feelings of guilt or pressure can be one of the most challenging parts of setting boundaries. But remember, your responsibility is first to yourself and your child. It is justified if a boundary is necessary for your well-being or your child's, regardless of any guilt or pressure you might face.

Should a family member argue, "We never had to set such boundaries in our time," you could respond, "I understand that times were different then, but this is what feels right for me and my child in our current situation."

In the grand scheme of things, setting boundaries is a part of your journey as a single parent. There will be moments of discomfort and periods of adjustment. But ultimately, setting healthy boundaries will help cultivate a nurturing environment where you, your child, and your extended family can have meaningful and respectful relationships.

Handling Family Conflict and Criticism

While navigating single parenthood, conflict and criticism from extended family and in-laws can seem like an unavoidable hurdle. Everyone has an opinion, and sometimes these opinions may not align with your parenting approach. However, you can handle these situations adeptly with effective communication strategies and a strong sense of self-confidence. This section delves into actionable strategies for managing family conflict and criticism.

Understanding the Source

Recognize that criticism often stems from concern, cultural norms, or personal experiences. Understanding the root of the criticism can help you empathize with the critic while formulating a thoughtful response. Avoid taking criticism personally; instead, view it as an opportunity to strengthen your resolve and improve your communication skills.

Active Listening

When criticism or conflict arises, the first step is to listen. Active listening enables you to fully understand the other party's perspective and respond thoughtfully. It involves giving your undivided attention, demonstrating understanding through body language, and occasionally paraphrasing your points to confirm comprehension.

Constructive Response

Responding to criticism is a delicate art. When crafting your response, be assertive without being defensive. Clearly express your standpoint using "I" statements to avoid escalating the conflict. For instance, instead of saying, "You're wrong," try, "I understand your perspective, but I see things differently."

Conflict Resolution

If criticism escalates to conflict, aim for resolution over victory. Seek compromise where possible. Use phrases like "Let's find a solution that works for both of us" to foster collaboration. If tensions run high, involving a neutral third party or seeking professional guidance might be beneficial.

Building Self-confidence

Criticism can take a toll on your self-confidence. Remember, you are the parent, and you are capable. Learn to trust your instincts and decision-making ability. Self-confidence is like a shield that can help you handle criticism and conflict more effectively.

In handling criticism and conflict, some additional tips include:

Avoid heated confrontations: Escalating conflicts rarely lead to productive outcomes. If a conversation becomes heated, take a break and revisit the discussion when all parties are calmer.

Decide what deserves your attention: Not all criticism must be addressed; some may not be worth your time or emotional energy.

Practice self-care: Handling criticism and conflict can be mentally draining.

Ensure you're taking time for self-care. This might involve activities that relax or reenergize you, like yoga, reading, or spending time in nature.

Keep your child's best interests at heart: When criticisms or conflicts revolve around your child, always consider what's best for them. As their parent, your primary responsibility is their well-being.

Handling family conflict and criticism is a challenging aspect of single parenting and an opportunity for growth. It can refine your communication skills, build resilience, and even strengthen your relationships with family members. Remember, every challenge you overcome is a testament to your strength as a parent.

Let's explore some common scenarios you might encounter as a single parent and how to handle them effectively.

Scenario 1: Undermining Your Parenting Decisions

When a family member contradicts or undermines your parenting decisions, addressing the issue directly yet respectfully is crucial. For example, if a relative continuously disregards your rules about screen time, you might say, "I understand you have your perspective, but I've set these rules for my child's wellbeing. I would appreciate it if you could respect them."

Scenario 2: Unsolicited Advice

Family members often mean well when they offer advice, but it can feel intrusive or judgmental. You might respond, "I appreciate your concern and willingness to share your experiences. But as my child's parent, I must make the best decisions for us."

Scenario 3: Incessant Criticism

Sometimes, a family member might become a constant source of criticism, nitpicking your parenting style or decisions. Address this by expressing how these criticisms make you feel. For example, "When you constantly criticize my parenting, it makes me feel undermined. I'm doing my best and would appreciate your support instead."

Scenario 4: Conflicts over Visitations or Custody

Conflicts over visitation or custody arrangements can be particularly challenging. If you find yourself in this situation, involving legal counsel or a mediator may be beneficial to ensure the resolution is fair and in your child's best interests.

In all scenarios, remember to:

Maintain your composure: Keep your emotions in check when addressing criticism or conflict. This model's good conflict resolution for your child prevents the situation from escalating.

Reiterate your boundaries: If criticism or conflict arises from overstepping boundaries, remind your family members of these boundaries and the importance of respecting them.

Prioritize your child: Your child's emotional and psychological well-being should always be the top priority. Ensure they feel loved, secure, and somewhat shielded from familial conflicts.

Conflict and criticism can be challenging, but remember; you are not alone. Many single parents face similar issues, and numerous resources are available to help them, including support groups, counseling services, and books. With perseverance, patience, and grace, you can manage familial conflicts and criticisms, turning them into opportunities for growth and strengthening bonds.

Creating a Nurturing and Stable Home Environment

In a child's world, home is their haven, where they can feel loved, nurtured, and secure. As a single parent, creating a nurturing and stable home environment may seem like a daunting task, but it's an essential component of successful single parenting. A positive home environment doesn't just provide physical safety for your child; it also fosters their emotional well-being, influences their behavior, and shapes their future.

Consistent Routine: Consistency is one of the best ways to establish stability in your home. This involves setting regular times for meals, homework, play, and bedtime. A predictable routine gives your child a sense of security and helps them understand what to expect each day.

Open Communication: Fostering open communication is crucial for creating a nurturing home environment. Encourage your child to express their thoughts and feelings and listen attentively when they do. Regularly check in to know how they are doing and show them their voice matters.

Display of Affection: Affection is vital in nurturing your child's emotional health. Regular hugs, kisses, and words of affirmation can significantly impact your child's self-esteem and sense of security.

Healthy Boundaries: Healthy boundaries are essential for creating a stable home environment. These boundaries help your child understand their limits and teach them respect for themselves and others.

Positive Atmosphere: Strive to maintain a positive atmosphere in your home. This doesn't mean ignoring problems or challenges but promoting a solution-focused mindset. Celebrate achievements, big or small, and foster a sense of optimism.

Role Modeling: As a single parent, you are your child's primary role model. They learn by observing your actions more than listening to your words. Show them how to handle emotions, resolve conflicts, and treat others with kindness and respect through your behavior.

Balance: While providing structure and set rules is important, maintaining a balance is equally important. Allow room for fun, relaxation, and spontaneity to ensure your home isn't just a place of rules and routine but also a place of joy and warmth.

Creating a nurturing and stable home environment lays the foundation for your child's mental and emotional health. It helps them feel secure and loved, which, in turn, supports their overall growth and development.

Promoting Social Skills and Friendships

Social skills are a fundamental part of a child's development. These skills, which include effective communication, empathy, problem-solving, and conflict resolution, help children navigate their relationships with peers, teachers, and, eventually, colleagues. Similarly, friendships play a vital role in your child's life, providing emotional support, opportunities for growth, and a sense of belonging. As a single parent, you can help nurture these skills and relationships in several ways.

Encourage Interaction: Provide opportunities for your child to interact with peers. This could be through play dates, joining clubs or sports teams, or participating in community events. These interactions allow your child to practice social skills in real-life situations.

Model Positive Interactions: Children learn a lot from observing the behavior of adults around them. Show them how to interact positively with others by demonstrating respectful communication, active listening, and empathy in your daily interactions.

Teach Conflict Resolution: Disagreements and conflicts are a natural part of any relationship. Teach your child how to handle conflicts healthily. This includes expressing feelings appropriately, listening to the other person's viewpoint, and finding a compromise.

Promote Empathy: Encourage your child to think about the feelings and perspectives of others. This could be through discussing characters in a book or movie or situations at school or home. Understanding others' feelings is a crucial aspect of forming strong friendships.

Support Their Friendships: Show interest in your child's friends and support these relationships. This could mean hosting play dates, driving them to activities, or simply asking about their friends and showing genuine interest.

Talk About Friendship Qualities: Have conversations about what makes a good friend. Highlight the importance of kindness, honesty, respect, and reliability.

Reinforce Positive Behavior: When you see your child demonstrating good social skills or being a good friend, acknowledge it. Positive reinforcement can strengthen these behaviors and encourage your child to repeat them.

Promoting social skills and friendships is an ongoing process. Still, the effort you put into this aspect of your child's development can impact their ability to form and maintain healthy relationships throughout their life.

Teaching Your Child about Respect and Values

The Importance of Respect and Values

Respect and values are integral elements of character development in children. Respect, which involves understanding and accepting the rights, beliefs, and opinions of others, builds a foundation for empathy, tolerance, and harmony. On the other hand, values guide behavior and decision-making, shaping your child's personality and character. As a single parent, teaching respect and instilling values in your child is a crucial responsibility.

How to Teach Respect

Teaching respect begins with your actions. Children are highly observant and tend to model their behavior after the adults in their lives. Therefore, demonstrating respect in your interactions with others can effectively teach your child about respect.

Modeling Respectful Behavior: Show respect in your daily interactions with others. This includes listening when others speak, acknowledging different viewpoints, and treating people with kindness and fairness.

Discussing Respect: Regularly engage your child in conversations about respect. Discuss what it means to be respectful, why it's important, and how to show respect to others.

Reinforcing Respectful Behavior: When you see your child behaving respectfully, acknowledge it. Positive reinforcement can be a powerful tool in encouraging respectful behavior.

Instilling Values

Values are deeply held beliefs that guide our actions and decisions and form the moral compass that helps us differentiate between right and wrong. As a parent, you play a critical role in instilling these values in your child.

Living Your Values: Your daily actions and decisions are the most potent lessons for your child. Live following the values you want your child to embrace, such as honesty, responsibility, kindness, and integrity.

Discussing Values: Engage your child in conversations about values. Discuss different situations and the values that could guide decisions and actions in these situations.

Reinforcing Values: Reinforce the importance of values through positive reinforcement. Praise your child when they demonstrate the values you've been teaching.

Teaching respect and instilling values can be challenging, but the impact on your child's character and behavior is well worth the effort. In the next chapter, we'll explore strategies for self-care and maintaining your mental health as a single parent, which is just as important as any other aspect of your parenting journey.

13. Single Parenting Through Different Stages of Childhood

In the grand journey of single parenting, each stage of your child's growth introduces new adventures, challenges, and moments of joy. From the first moments of infancy to the trials and triumphs of the teenage years, each phase of your child's development offers unique opportunities for bonding, learning, and mutual growth. This chapter delves into the nuances of single parenting through the different stages of childhood—infancy, toddlerhood, elementary school, and the tumultuous yet transformative phase of adolescence and the teen years.

Being a single parent often feels like a superhero juggling a dynamic range of tasks and emotions simultaneously. The role can be exhausting and challenging yet deeply rewarding. Understanding and preparing for each phase of your child's growth can equip you with the insights, strategies, and confidence you need to navigate these stages effectively.

By appreciating each stage's distinct needs, potentials, and challenges, you can better support your child's development and foster a deep, meaningful, and lasting bond with them. Let's embark on this exploration, starting with the earliest stages of childhood—infancy and toddlerhood.

Parenting Infants and Toddlers

The first stage of childhood, encompassing infancy and toddlerhood, is a magical time filled with rapid growth, discovery, and foundational development. During this stage, your child depends on you for their basic needs, emotional comfort, and social interaction. As a single parent, you can shape your child's earliest experiences and foster a nurturing, stimulating environment.

Nurturing the Bond

Infancy and toddlerhood are crucial periods for bonding with your child. This is when your child begins to recognize you as their primary caregiver, source of comfort, and guide to the world. Create routines promoting close physical contacts, such as breastfeeding, bottle-feeding, or bedtime rituals.

Simple acts like holding, cuddling, or rocking your baby can strengthen your emotional connection and give your infant a sense of security.

Understanding Developmental Milestones

During these early years, your child will achieve significant developmental milestones, including physical growth, motor skills development, and cognitive advancement. Familiarize yourself with these milestones to better understand your child's growth and anticipate their evolving needs. Remember, each child develops at their own pace, so use these milestones as guides rather than stringent benchmarks.

Providing a Stimulating Environment

The world is a wonder-filled playground for infants and toddlers waiting to be explored. Encourage their curiosity by providing a stimulating environment. This could include age-appropriate toys, picture books, or sensory activities. Talk to your child regularly, narrate your activities, and respond to their coos and babbles. These interactions will foster their cognitive and language development.

Establishing Routines and Structure

Routines provide infants and toddlers with a sense of security and predictability. Establishing regular patterns for meals, naps, playtime, and bedtime can help soothe your child and regulate their behavior. However, maintain flexibility in your routines to accommodate your child's changing needs and unexpected situations.

Self-Care and Seeking Support

Parenting an infant or toddler as a single parent can be physically and emotionally demanding. Remember to care for your own needs too. Establish a self-care routine, seek help from friends, family, or professional caregivers when needed, and connect with other single parents for mutual support and advice.

Navigating Challenges and Celebrating Milestones

Like every stage of parenting, infancy and toddlerhood come with their challenges—sleep disruptions, feeding difficulties, or temper tantrums. Approach these challenges with patience, empathy, and a problem-solving mindset. Remember, these hurdles are also opportunities for learning and growth—for you and your child. Amid these challenges, don't forget to celebrate the milestones, the firsts, and the everyday moments of joy.

Preparing for the Next Stage

As your child approaches the end of their toddler years, prepare for the next phase of childhood—the elementary school years. This transition can change your child's independence, social interactions, and learning needs. As you cherish the remaining moments of toddlerhood, also look forward to the growth and exploration that the coming years promise.

Parenting infants and toddlers as a single parent is a unique journey filled with joy, challenges, and immeasurable love. Embrace this journey with patience, empathy, and understanding, and cherish the precious moments of growth, discovery, and bonding it brings.

Prioritizing Safety

Creating a safe environment for your infant or toddler is paramount. Childproof your home to minimize potential hazards—secure heavy furniture, block access to stairs, lock cabinets that contain cleaning supplies or medicines, and keep small objects out of reach. It's also essential to ensure car safety by using appropriate child car seats. Monitor product recalls and safety warnings for child products and toys. Familiarize yourself with infant and toddler first aid, and consider taking a CPR class.

Encouraging Healthy Eating Habits

This stage also marks the introduction of solid foods and the formation of early eating habits. Gradually introduce various healthy foods, and encourage self-feeding as your toddler grows. Patience is critical during this transition—messes and resistance to new foods might occur. It's all a part of the learning process.

Building Early Literacy Skills

Even in infancy and toddlerhood, you can nurture early literacy skills. Read to your child regularly, pointing out pictures and engaging them with your voice. Make books a part of your daily routines, such as before bedtime. This early exposure to books and reading can instill a lifelong love for learning.

Instilling Healthy Sleep Habits

Sleep is fundamental to your child's growth and development. Establish a bedtime routine and a consistent sleep schedule. Create a calm, comforting sleep environment and use consistent cues that signal it's time to sleep. Understanding your child's sleep needs and patterns can also help prevent overstimulation and overtiredness.

Developing Social Skills

Though your child's social circle is limited during this stage, early social skills develop. Interact with your child, respond to their cues, and encourage simple social games like peekaboo or mimicry activities. Expose them to various social situations and people to help them become comfortable with social interactions.

Nurturing Emotional Development

Emotional development is a critical aspect of your child's early years. Validate their emotions, help them name their feelings, and guide them toward managing these emotions. Modeling healthy emotional expression and responsiveness contributes significantly to your child's emotional growth.

In these early years, single parenting is a journey of unconditional love, ceaseless dedication, and constant growth. Significant milestones, delightful discoveries, and precious bonding moments mark it. It might be challenging at times, but the joy of witnessing your child's first steps, words, and ever-evolving curiosity make it a wonderfully rewarding journey. Cherish this special time as you lay the foundation for your child's future and build a bond that will last a lifetime.

The Elementary School Years

The transition from toddlerhood to the elementary school years signifies a time of immense growth and discovery. Your child's increasing independence characterizes this period, the formation of their identity, the expansion of their social world, and their intellectual development. As a single parent, guiding your child through these transformative years can be as challenging as rewarding.

During these years, your role evolves from a primary caregiver to a guide, supporting your child as they navigate new experiences, build relationships, and gain knowledge. This stage demands a shift in parenting strategies—focusing more on communication, education, discipline, and social-emotional development.

Navigating the First Day of School

The first day of school is a significant milestone, filled with excitement and apprehension—for you and your child. Prepare your child for this big day by discussing what to expect, touring the school if possible, and encouraging a positive attitude towards school.

Reinforce the idea that a school is a place for learning, making friends, and having fun. After the first day, discuss their experiences, address their concerns, and celebrate this milestone.

Fostering a Love for Learning

One of your key roles during this stage is to instill a love for learning. Encourage curiosity, creativity, and critical thinking. Show enthusiasm about their education, involve yourself in their homework and school projects, and foster a home environment that values knowledge and curiosity. However, ensure you push them appropriately, maintaining a healthy balance between learning and play.

Encouraging Social Skills and Friendships

The elementary school years mark the expansion of your child's social circle. They begin forming friendships, understanding social norms, and navigating social situations. Encourage them to make friends, but also teach them about the qualities of a good friend. Discuss situations of peer pressure, bullying, and conflict, equipping them with strategies to handle them.

Implementing Effective Discipline

As your child grows more independent, they may test boundaries, requiring the implementation of effective discipline strategies. Set clear expectations, be consistent with consequences, and use these moments as learning opportunities. Most importantly, remember to reinforce positive behavior.

Promoting Healthy Habits

During the elementary school years, children continue to develop habits and routines that can have lasting impacts on their health and wellness. Encourage a balanced diet, regular physical activity, and a consistent sleep schedule. Also, foster good hygiene habits and teach them about the importance of personal care.

Nurturing Emotional Intelligence

Emotional intelligence—the ability to understand, manage, and express emotions—becomes increasingly important during this stage. Help your child identify and articulate feelings, empathize with others, and develop coping strategies for difficult emotions. Your emotional intelligence demonstration can be a powerful model for your child.

Encouraging Independence

As your child matures, encourage independence by assigning age-appropriate responsibilities and allowing them to make certain decisions. This could involve household chores, managing homework, or choosing outfits. Foster a sense of self-reliance but be there to guide and support when necessary.

Building Self-Esteem

During these formative years, your child develops a sense of self-worth. Praise their efforts, acknowledge their achievements, and encourage their unique interests and skills. However, also help them navigate failures and disappointments, teaching them resilience and the value of perseverance.

Preparing for Adolescence

As the elementary school years close, your child stands at the brink of adolescence a period of even more significant transformations. Start conversations about body changes, the dynamics of peer relationships, the pressures and challenges of the teenage years, and the importance of open communication.

While marked by remarkable growth and change, the elementary school years also bring unique challenges and milestones for you and your child. As a single parent, you play a pivotal role in guiding your child through these transformative years. Remember, your love, support, and understanding provide the stability and reassurance your child needs as they navigate this significant phase of their life. Embrace the challenges, celebrate the milestones, and treasure the shared experiences these years bring.

Navigating Adolescence and the Teen Years

The journey of single parenting takes a significant turn as your child enters adolescence and the teen years. This stage, often regarded as one of the most challenging periods of parenting, is marked by your child's physical maturation, emotional turmoil, cognitive development, and social expansion. These changes come with new challenges—identity, autonomy, peer pressure, academic expectations, and, sometimes, risk-taking behaviors.

As a single parent, guiding your child through these turbulent years can sometimes feel overwhelming. However, this period also offers profound opportunities for connection, growth, and deepening mutual understanding. It's a time when your child's identity takes shape, their worldview expands, and their dreams for the future become more concrete. Let's delve into the strategies and insights to help you navigate adolescence and teen years with confidence and empathy.

Understanding Adolescent Development

Adolescence is a period of significant physical, emotional, and cognitive development. Understanding these changes can help you empathize with your teen and respond effectively to their needs. Discuss these changes openly with your teen and reassure them that these transitions are a normal part of growing up.

Encouraging Open Communication

Keeping lines of communication open is critical during the teen years. Encourage your teen to express their thoughts, feelings, and concerns. Be an active listener, show empathy, and provide guidance when needed. Regular conversations about their daily life, friendships, challenges, and aspirations can strengthen your bond and offer valuable insights into their world.

Setting Boundaries and Implementing Discipline

Setting clear and reasonable boundaries becomes crucial as your teen seeks more independence. Discuss these boundaries, involve your teen in setting rules, and ensure they understand the consequences of crossing these limits. Be firm but fair in implementing discipline.

Nurturing Self-Esteem and Identity

During adolescence, your teen develops their identity and sense of self. Encourage their unique interests, talents, and values. Support them as they explore their identity and validate their feelings and experiences. Foster a positive self-image and resilience to help them navigate the ups and downs of adolescence.

Promoting Healthy Lifestyle Choices

Teens are often confronted with choices about substance use, sexual activity, and health behaviors. Engage in honest, open discussions about these topics. Educate them about risks, encourage healthy choices, and ensure they can turn to you for guidance and support.

Supporting Academic Goals and Career Exploration

The teen years are a critical time for academic growth and career exploration. Support your teen's academic goals, encourage a strong work ethic, and help them explore potential career paths. Offer guidance but allow them the space to make decisions about their future.

Preparing for Adulthood

As your teen grows older, discussions about adulthood become increasingly important. Talk about financial responsibility, independent living skills, and emotional maturity. Equip them with the tools they need to transition into adulthood successfully.

Navigating adolescence and the teen years as a single parent may present unique challenges. However, you can support your teen through these transformative years with empathy, understanding, and effective communication. As you guide them towards adulthood, cherish the shared moments of growth, the deep conversations, and the strengthening of your bond that these years bring.

14. Envisioning the Future

As your children grow, so will your role as a single parent. The years will shift like sand beneath your feet, carrying you from the whirlwind days of early childhood to the breathtaking precipice of adulthood. This chapter is about that journey – a journey not just for your children but for you as well. "Envisioning the Future" is about acknowledging the inherent fluidity of the parenting role, preparing for the various transitions, and, most importantly, ensuring that you are prepared for the next phase of your life.

While the earlier chapters of this book focused on immediate strategies and coping mechanisms, this one encourages you to take a more comprehensive, more long-term view. It's a chapter that urges you to consider the evolution of your single parenting role and your life beyond it. From preparing for your child's college and career, dealing with the impending 'empty nest' syndrome, to reflecting on your journey and planning for retirement.

This chapter is a gentle reminder that the essence of single parenting isn't merely about the present; it's about envisioning the future. It's about planting seeds today that will grow into strong trees tomorrow - both for your children and for yourself.

Preparing for Your Child's College and Career

Our journey begins with looking ahead to your child's entrance into college and the start of their career. In these pivotal years, your role as a parent morphs into something new. No longer are you the all-knowing figure that you were in their childhood; now, you transition into the role of a trusted guide, a compass to help them navigate these new, uncharted waters.

Perhaps you need to be more apprehensive. The prospect of college and careers may seem distant and daunting, especially when your child is still navigating high school. The leap from adolescence to adulthood, from high school to college, and from there to a professional career can seem like an insurmountable chasm. But remember, you're not alone, and this transition doesn't have to be a leap—it can be a series of small, manageable steps.

As you start, remember that preparing your child for college isn't just about academics. It's about equipping them with the social, emotional, and financial skills they need to thrive in a rapidly changing world. It teaches them resilience, independence, and a sense of responsibility. Talk to them about the importance of setting goals and making a plan. Walk them through the process of exploring various career paths, applying for college, and understanding the practicalities of managing finances.

Exploring Their Interests

Every child is unique with their passions and aptitudes, which will often play a significant role in the direction they choose for their future. As a single parent, one of your responsibilities is to help them identify these interests and nurture them. This could be through educational outings, reading books, or discussing their thoughts and dreams. It's about offering them opportunities to explore their natural inclinations while encouraging them to broaden their horizons.

Remember, it's not about imposing your aspirations or dreams on them but about supporting them in discovering who they are and what they enjoy. Be mindful of their strengths, respect their choices, and help them understand that the path to a fulfilling career is not necessarily linear.

Guiding Their Academic Journey

As your child progresses through school, their academic journey will begin to have more tangible implications for their future. At this stage, you'll be required to balance your role as a guide, helping them to make informed decisions about subject choices, course levels, and college applications, with your role as a parent, providing emotional support and reassurance.

Keeping current with college admission processes, financial aid opportunities, and scholarship programs can seem daunting, but many resources are available. Talk to your child's school guidance counselor, contact local community organizations, and use online platforms dedicated to helping parents and students navigate this process.

Supporting Their Decisions

As your child decides about their future, offering your support is important. This doesn't mean you can't express your concerns or share your opinions; they must benefit from your experience and wisdom. However, it does mean respecting their autonomy and allowing them to take responsibility for their choices.

In supporting your child's decisions, you're fostering their independence and resilience - essential qualities they'll need as they enter adulthood. You're showing them that you trust their judgment, which will significantly improve their self-confidence.

Fostering Lifelong Skills

In addition to the academic and career-related aspects, preparing your child for the practical side of life is equally important. This could involve teaching them how to manage their finances, do laundry, cook nutritious meals, or use public transportation.

While seemingly mundane, these skills can significantly ease the transition to college or work life. They also contribute to your child's overall self-sufficiency, empowering them to navigate the world confidently and competently.

Preparing for your child's college and career isn't simply about academics or professions; it's about fostering their growth as individuals, guiding them through decisions, and empowering them with practical life skills. It's about supporting them as they map their unique future path.

Understanding the Financial Landscape

As a single parent, grappling with the financial implications of your child's higher education can be overwhelming. But don't let this deter you. Understanding the financial landscape, exploring options, and planning can go a long way in mitigating stress: research tuition fees, living expenses, and potential financial aid options. There are a multitude of scholarships, grants, and work-study programs that your child may be eligible for.

It's also beneficial to involve your child in this process. This offers them a practical insight into financial management, the value of money, and the importance of planning and saving. If the costs of their dream education seem formidable, encourage them to consider alternatives such as attending a community college first or studying part-time while working. The goal is to nurture their ambitions while instilling a sense of financial responsibility.

Cultivating Emotional Resilience

Preparing for college and a career isn't just about academics, practical skills, or finances, it's also about cultivating emotional resilience. As they step into this new chapter of their lives, their child will inevitably face challenges, uncertainties, and failures. Helping them develop coping mechanisms, self-care practices, and mental strength is crucial.

Ensure that they know it's okay to ask for help and that seeking emotional, psychological, or academic support is not a sign of weakness but strength. Teach them that failure is an inevitable part of life and growth and that each setback is a stepping stone toward success. Foster a growth mindset that encourages perseverance, adaptability, and resilience.

Balancing Your Roles

Remember to balance your roles as you guide your child through this transformative period. While you're their guide, you're also their parent. Maintain an open line of communication, provide a safe space to express their fears, hopes, and dreams, and offer them unconditional love and support.

You may experience a range of emotions as you prepare your child for their future: pride in their growth, anxiety about their choices, and perhaps even a tinge of sadness as you perceive them stepping away from the nest. It's important to acknowledge these feelings and permit yourself to experience them. Just as your child is growing and evolving, so are you.

Finally, remember that while preparing your child for college and career is crucial, it is equally important to enjoy the present. Cherish your time with your child now, celebrate their achievements, share in their excitement, and revel in the joy of seeing them bloom into their full potential.

The Empty Nest: Life After Your Child Leaves Home

The day you drop your child off at their college dormitory or first apartment is momentous. It's the culmination of years of late-night homework help, packed lunches, shared laughter, occasional tears, and countless moments of learning and growth. As you hug them goodbye, you feel a swirl of emotions: immense pride, a twinge of sadness, a sense of accomplishment, and perhaps, a quiet, lurking apprehension. Once filled with their presence, your home is about to become quieter, a little emptier - a signal of a significant shift in your life as a parent. You're facing the 'empty nest' stage.

The empty nest period can be challenging, particularly for single parents who have dedicated much of their lives to their children. This chapter focuses on understanding and navigating this transition effectively. It covers various topics, from managing the initial feelings of loss and redefining your identity to rediscovering your interests and hobbies, nurturing your social connections, and planning for your next life phase. It's about reframing this change not as an end but as the beginning of an exciting new journey.

The essence of this chapter is to help you transition gracefully from a hands-on parent to a long-distance cheerleader, from an everyday guide to an occasional advisor. It's about reassessing and redefining your role as a parent and individual. It's about embracing the freedom, independence, and opportunities of an empty nest while maintaining your bond and connection with your child.

Processing the Transition

The initial days and weeks after your child leaves home may feel strange and difficult. The house may feel too quiet, too clean, or too big. The routines you've become accustomed to—preparing meals, helping with homework, attending school events—have suddenly disappeared, replaced by a new rhythm that may seem unfamiliar and disturbing.

Recognize that these feelings are normal. It's okay to feel a sense of loss or sadness; it's okay to miss your child's daily presence. But it's also important to remember that this isn't an end but a transition—a shift in the dynamics of your relationship with your child, a move towards a new chapter of your life.

Redefining Your Identity

For years, your identity has been largely tied to being a parent, specifically, a single parent. Now, as your child embarks on their journey, it's time to redefine your identity. This might involve reassessing your interests, hobbies, career, or personal goals. Maybe you've wanted to travel, write a book, return to school, or volunteer. Perhaps there's a project at work that you've been eager to tackle, or maybe there's a hobby you'd love to revisit. Now is your chance.

It's essential to remember that you're not just a parent; you're an individual with your dreams, ambitions, and passions. Use this transition period as an opportunity to rediscover and redefine yourself.

Cultivating Your Interests and Hobbies

With your child no longer occupying the majority of your time, you'll find yourself with hours that you can dedicate to your interests. Did you use to paint before the pressures of single parenting took over? Maybe you enjoyed hiking or were passionate about cooking or gardening.

Revisit these hobbies. Join clubs or groups that align with your interests. The aim is to fill your life with activities that you find fulfilling and enjoyable, helping you build a new routine around your interests.

Nurturing Social Connections

Social connections are crucial, especially during transitional periods in our lives. Contact your friends, join social groups, participate in community events, or consider volunteering. Not only will this keep you socially engaged, but it'll also offer a sense of purpose and community. If you feel ready, consider exploring the dating scene. The idea is to build a social network outside your parent role.

While challenging, The empty nest period presents a unique opportunity to focus on yourself. It's a chance to rediscover who you are outside your parental role, explore your passions, nurture your social connections, and build a fulfilling and enriching life. It's about stepping into a new phase of your life with excitement, anticipation, and grace.

Reflecting on Your Single Parenting Journey

The journey of single parenting is monumental, marked by trials and triumphs, challenges and victories, laughter and tears. It's a journey that tests your strength, resilience, and resourcefulness. As your child steps into adulthood and you move into the 'empty nest' phase, it's beneficial to reflect on this journey - to look back on the path you've traversed, the mountains you've scaled, and the rivers you've crossed.

Take a moment to appreciate the journey you've been on. Recognize the courage it took to raise a child alone, the sacrifices you've made, and the countless moments of love, joy, and growth you've shared with your child. Reminisce about the birthdays; the school plays the late-night conversations, the shared dreams, and the tender hugs. Treasure these moments, for they have shaped you and your child in more ways than one.

Lessons Learned

Your single parenting journey has undoubtedly taught you valuable lessons. Perhaps you've learned about the strength of your spirit, the depth of your love, the extent of your patience, or the power of your resilience. Maybe you've discovered new skills, picked up useful strategies, or developed effective coping mechanisms. Reflect on these lessons, cherish them, and see how they have shaped your identity and perspective.

However, it's not just about the lessons you've learned but also about the lessons you've imparted to your child. As a single parent, you've shown them the essence of independence, the power of perseverance, and the strength of character. You've taught them about resilience, adaptability, and courage. Reflect on these lessons and recognize your role in shaping your child's values, personality, and outlook on life.

Overcoming Regrets

No journey is devoid of regrets or 'what if's, and the parenting journey is no exception. Maybe there were moments you wish you had handled differently, decisions you regret making, or opportunities you wish you had seized. It's natural to harbor such feelings, but it's also essential to remember that parenting is an intricate dance of trial and error, learning, and growing.

Acknowledge your regrets, but don't let them overshadow your accomplishments. Understand that you did the best you could with the resources, knowledge, and circumstances you had at that time. Allow these regrets to be stepping stones for growth and learning rather than weights pulling you down.

Gratitude and Joy

Finally, reflect on the joy and fulfillment of single parenting. Yes, there were challenges and hardships, but moments of profound joy made your heart swell with love and pride. There were times when your child's laughter filled your home, their achievements brought tears to your eyes, and their love wrapped you in warmth. Gratitude can be a powerful lens through which to view your journey.

Reflecting on your single parenting journey is about more than just reminiscing. It's about cherishing experiences, recognizing growth, learning from regrets, and expressing gratitude for joy and fulfillment. It's about appreciating the strength, love, and resilience that have been the cornerstones of your journey and carrying these attributes forward into the next chapter of your life.

Acknowledging Personal Growth

Throughout your single parenting journey, you've grown in numerous ways. You've become more resilient, adaptable, patient, and resourceful. You've learned to navigate challenges, make difficult decisions, and juggle multiple roles. You've become a master of time management, budgeting, multitasking, and problem-solving.

Reflecting on these areas of growth helps to remind you of your strength and capability and provides a source of motivation and inspiration for the future. It's a reminder of how far you've come and the myriad skills and qualities you've developed on this journey.

Honoring Your Resilience

Resilience is a hallmark of single parenting. You've weathered storms, overcome obstacles, and bounced back from setbacks. You've shown your child that facing adversity head-on is possible and coming out stronger on the other side.

As you reflect on your journey, honor this resilience. Recognize it as a testament to your strength, courage, and tenacious spirit. This resilience will continue to serve you in the 'empty nest' phase and beyond. It's a quality that will empower you to face future challenges, seize new opportunities, and continue growing and evolving.

Planning for Retirement as a Single Parent

As you move into the 'empty nest' stage, it's time to start planning for retirement. This involves envisioning the life you want to lead once you stop working full-time. Do you dream of traveling the world, dedicating yourself to a particular hobby, volunteering for a passionate cause, or spending quality time with your loved ones?

Take some time to visualize your retirement. Consider your aspirations, lifestyle, health, and financial situation. The more precise you are about your retirement goals, the better you can plan for them.

Assessing Your Financial Status

A key aspect of retirement planning is assessing your current financial status. How much have you saved? Do you have any debts or liabilities? What are your sources of income?

Consider seeking the advice of a financial planner or consultant to help you understand your financial situation better. They can provide valuable guidance on optimizing your savings, managing your debts, and planning your investments. Remember, the aim is to save for retirement and build a nest egg to live comfortably and fulfill your retirement dreams.

Building a Retirement Budget

Once you understand your financial status and retirement goals, you can start building a retirement budget. This budget should include all your expected expenses, such as living, healthcare, travel, and any other expenses related to your retirement goals.

Again, a financial advisor can be of great help here. They can help you estimate your expenses, suggest ways to minimize costs, and guide you on how to make your savings last through retirement.

Understanding Your Pension and Social Security Benefits

As a single parent, it's crucial to understand your pension and social security benefits. These can be significant sources of income during your retirement. If you need clarification on these benefits, consider consulting a financial advisor or a social security office.

Preparing for Healthcare Needs

Healthcare is a critical consideration in retirement planning, especially as healthcare needs increase. Consider factors like health insurance, long-term care costs, and out-of-pocket expenses. Look into options like Medicare, supplemental, and long-term care insurance.

Embracing Life-Long Learning and Personal Growth

Retirement is not just about financial planning but also personal growth and fulfillment. It's a phase of life that offers the time and freedom to learn new skills, pursue hobbies, and embrace new experiences. As you plan for retirement, consider how you want to continue growing and evolving as an individual.

Planning for retirement as a single parent can seem daunting, but with careful planning, financial savvy, and a clear vision, you can confidently navigate this journey. Remember, retirement is not an end but a new, exciting chapter of life that promises personal growth, relaxation, and fulfillment.

Conclusion

The journey of single parenting is as rewarding as it is challenging. It is an expedition full of moments that test your resilience, patience, and spirit yet also bestow upon you an immeasurable depth of love and growth. As we conclude this book, it's important to remember that every single parent's journey is unique and consists of diverse experiences, trials, triumphs, and individual lessons. However, what unites all single parents is the shared love for their children and the commitment to nurturing them.

In traversing this journey, you've played the role of both parents, providing financial stability, emotional support, academic assistance, moral guidance, and unconditional love. You've been a cheerleader, a teacher, a confidant, and a guide. Most importantly, you've been a pillar of strength, showing your child the power of resilience, the significance of independence, and the value of perseverance.

You have played an indispensable part in your child's growth and development. You've helped shape their values, mold their character, and influence their outlook on life. As they enter adulthood, they carry forward the lessons they've learned from you—the essence of self-reliance, the power of resilience, the importance of integrity, and the virtue of kindness. These lessons will guide them as they navigate their journeys, helping them grow into responsible, compassionate, and successful adults.

The 'empty nest' stage and retirement planning, the focal points of the final chapter of this book, mark significant transitions in your life as a single parent. They represent a shift in your role as a parent, a change in your daily routines, and a new phase of your journey. While challenging, these stages also offer immense opportunities—for personal growth, self-exploration, social engagement, and financial planning.

Embrace these transitions. Look at them not with apprehension but with optimism and excitement. View them as opportunities to rediscover your identity, pursue your passions, nurture your social connections, and plan for a comfortable and fulfilling retirement. Remember, every transition in life is a new door opening a chance to explore new paths, seize new opportunities, and write new chapters in your life's story.

Ultimately, being a single parent isn't just about raising your child. It's about growing with them, learning from them, and evolving. It's about building a bond based on love, respect, trust, and mutual growth. It's about turning challenges into opportunities, trials into triumphs, and experiences into lessons. It's about finding joy in the journey and fulfillment in the role of a parent.

As we conclude, we salute you, the single parent, for your strength, resilience, dedication, and love. You've walked a challenging path with grace and determination, setting an example of courage and commitment for your child. You've shown them and the world that single parenting is not just about raising a child alone; it's about raising them with love, integrity, and resilience.

May this book have served as a companion to you on your journey, providing guidance, support, and reassurance. As you continue on your path, remember that you are not alone. A community of single parents is out there, sharing similar experiences, facing similar challenges, and celebrating similar triumphs. Lean on this community for support, share your experiences, learn from others, and contribute your insights.

In the end, remember that the journey of single parenting is not defined by the challenges it entails but by the love it embodies, the growth it fosters, and the lives it enriches. Keep moving forward, keep growing, and keep loving. You are not just a single parent but a beacon of strength, resilience, and a model of love.

Here's to you and the remarkable journey of single parenting. May your path be filled with love, joy, growth, and fulfillment. And may the future bring you and your child the best that life offers.

Printed in Great Britain
by Amazon